D0342812

THEotherAMERICA

GAY&LESBIAN Youth

These and other titles are included in *The Other America* series:

THE other AMERICA

GAY & LESBIAN Youth

by
Gail B. Stewart

Photographs by
Natasha Frost

Lucent Books, P.O. Box 289011, San Diego, CA 92198-9011

Cover design: Carl Franzen

Library of Congress Cataloging-in-Publication Data

Stewart, Gail, 1949–
    Gay and lesbian youth / by Gail B. Stewart; photographs by Natasha Frost.
       p. cm.—(The other America)
    Includes bibliographical references and index.
    Summary: First-person accounts of four homosexual Americans—three
teenagers and a twenty-year-old university student.
    ISBN 1-56006-337-8 (alk. paper)
    1. Gay youth—United States—Interviews—Juvenile literature. 2. Lesbian
youth—United States—Interviews—Juvenile literature. [1. Gays—Interviews.
2. Lesbians—Interviews. 3. Homosexuality.] I. Frost, Natasha, photog., 1974– .
II. Title. III. Series: Stewart, Gail, 1949– Other America.
HQ76.26.S74   1997
305.23′5′08664—dc20   96-27895
                                                 CIP
                                                AC

Printed in the U.S.A.
Copyright © 1997 by Lucent Books, Inc.
P.O. Box 289011, San Diego, CA 92198-9011

Contents

Foreword

O, YES,
I SAY IT PLAIN,
AMERICA NEVER WAS AMERICA TO ME.
AND YET I SWEAR THIS OATH—
AMERICA WILL BE!
LANGSTON HUGHES

Perhaps more than any other nation in the world, the United States represents an ideal to many people. The ideal of equality— of opportunity, of legal rights, of protection against discrimination and oppression. To a certain extent, this image has proven accurate. But beneath this ideal lies a less idealistic fact—many segments of our society do not feel included in this vision of America.

They are the outsiders—the homeless, the elderly, people with AIDS, teenage mothers, gang members, prisoners, and countless others. When politicians and the media discuss society's ills, the members of these groups are defined as what's wrong with America; they are the people who need fixing, who need help, or increasingly, who need to take more responsibility. And as these people become society's fix-it problem, they lose all identity as individuals and become part of an anonymous group. In the media and in our minds these groups are identified by condition—a disease, crime, morality, poverty. Their condition becomes their identity, and once this occurs, in the eyes of society, they lose their humanity.

The Other America series reveals the members of these groups as individuals. Through in-depth interviews, each person tells his or her unique story. At times these stories are painful, revealing individuals who are struggling to maintain their integrity, their humanity, their lives, in the face of fear, loss, and economic and spiritual hardship. At other times, their tales are exasperating, demonstrating a litany of poor choices, shortsighted thinking, and self-gratification. Nevertheless, their identities remain distinct, their personalities diverse.

As we listen to the people of *The Other America* series describe their experiences they cease to be stereotypically defined and become tangible, individual. In the process, we may begin to understand more profoundly and think more critically about society's problems. When politicians debate, for example, whether the homeless problem is due to a poor economy or lack of initiative, it will help to read the words of the homeless. Perhaps then we can see the issue more clearly. The family who finds itself temporarily homeless because it has always been one paycheck from poverty is not the same as the mother of six who has been chronically chemically dependent. These people's circumstances are not all of one kind, and perhaps we, after all, are not so very different from them. Before we can act to solve the problems of the Other America, we must be willing to look down their path, to see their faces. And perhaps in doing so, we may find a piece of ourselves as well.

Introduction

A fifteen-year-old Florida girl, a sophomore in high school, fatally shot herself with her father's target pistol. She left behind a letter to her parents and older sister, informing them that she was a lesbian. Although she had never acted on her sexual feelings, she wrote, she knew "as much as I know anything, I know I'm attracted to girls, not boys."

However, the letter was not merely an admission of her own homosexuality. It was a frustrated cry from someone who was experiencing abandonment and isolation. "I hate my life," she wrote, "and I don't know what I can do to change things. You don't want a lesbian for a daughter, and no one at my school would understand either. . . . Most days I don't even like myself. And how can I like myself when no one else does? I don't have anyone to talk to. I'm tired of lying and pretending."

"A HISTORY OF NON-UNDERSTANDING"

Between 10 and 12 percent of adolescents in America are lesbian or gay, and an overwhelming majority of them have experienced the kinds of feelings described by the teen in Florida. Not all of them take their own lives, of course, but a surprising number have experienced severe depression, loneliness, isolation, and hopelessness. Almost 65 percent of gay and lesbian youth polled in 1993 said that they had seriously considered suicide. And in fact, the Department of Health and Human Services estimated in 1989 that at least 30 percent of the completed youth suicides every year are committed by lesbian and gay youth.

"We have a history of non-understanding where gay and lesbian kids are concerned," says a St. Paul counselor who works with troubled teens. "I see it all the time. We as a society would like to say we're open and understanding to diversity. And maybe we are in some things—like you don't hear as many white people use *nigger* or other racial insults in public.

"But if we think we've really evolved, we're way off the mark. I've worked with lots of kids who get harassed on a daily basis just because of their sexual preference. And I'm not just talking other kids here. I'm talking teachers, who laugh along with the jokes and the harassment—especially when they're directed at gay teens. And these are teachers who would never consider making fun of Jewish kids or African-American kids. These teachers think nothing of calling gay kids fairies or fruits. Some even switch the boy's name to a more feminine sounding one—like Christine instead of Christopher. Sure, it's a big joke."

Social ridicule of gays and lesbians is certainly a long-standing tradition in America and Europe. In the eighteenth century anyone who exhibited homosexual behavior was believed to be committing a sin against God, and the punishment—usually death—was handled by the church. In the 1800s the medical profession decided that homosexuality, then believed to be a relatively new problem for society, was a curable illness. Doctors spent a great deal of time treating gay and lesbian people with electroshock therapy, hypnosis, and even a regimen of ice-cold showers six times a day!

DRAGGING SOCIETY INTO THE TWENTIETH CENTURY

Gradually the idea that homosexuality could be cured by doctors gave way to psychotherapy, which had the same goals. Psychotherapists tried to take homosexuals back to the events that led up to their decision to become gay or lesbian, then reverse the decision by isolating and analyzing it.

By the late twentieth century many of the old ideas about homosexuality had been challenged. Anthropologists, for instance, discovered that gays and lesbians existed in almost every culture and society, going back many centuries. In some cultures, such as ancient Greece or certain Native American tribes, homosexuality was completely acceptable.

By the late 1980s, homosexuality was no longer on the list of medical disorders recognized by the American Psychiatric Association. Medical professionals were reaching the conclusion that homosexuality was in part the result of a complicated mixture of factors occurring before birth: genetic, neurological, and hormonal.

STILL A PROBLEM FOR SOCIETY

Although health professionals have changed their opinions about homosexuality, a great many Americans still find it socially unacceptable. Even more difficult for them to understand are youth who, as one mother of a gay son says, "have chosen this perverted lifestyle." Many people still believe that homosexuality is a conscious choice, influenced by a person's environment.

To many gays and lesbians, especially those still in high school, such attitudes are both frustrating and infuriating. They insist they have not chosen any lifestyle, that their sexuality is simply part of who they are.

"Hey, if I could choose a lifestyle, does anyone really think that I would choose to live a life where I'd get taunted at school, or I'd lose most of my friends?" asks one sixteen-year-old boy who has recently confided in some friends and family members about his homosexuality. "I can't walk down the hall without someone whistling at me or yelling fag. My dad won't talk to me. And my mom thinks I'm gay because my cousin Ben is gay, and maybe he recruited me or something stupid like that. I don't know. Maybe someday things will be better—I'm hoping so—but now my life is a mess."

Counselors and others who work with gay and lesbian youth say that such feelings are not representative of just a small minority of gay teens but, rather, are extraordinarily common.

The director of a shelter for troubled youth in Chicago claims that for most gay and lesbian teens, "their being gay has been decreed by society as a badge of shame. They aren't allowed to feel that they are worthwhile or good. Hey, and forget about feeling pride in themselves! And this is a time in life when they want desperately to fit in, be like their peers. I mean, this is not like having a bad hair day, or braces, or the wrong kind of jeans. This is something that isn't going away; that's a key part of who they are."

A DANGEROUS WORLD

The world in which gay and lesbian youth live is fraught with danger. They are harassed and physically assaulted by others, a phenomenon called gay bashing. They are often isolated, having been cut off by family and friends. As a result, gay and lesbian youth are at far higher risk of experiencing severe depression and hopelessness. And, as mentioned before, their suicide rate is far higher than that of heterosexual youth.

"I worry about my son contracting AIDS or HIV," says the father of a Chicago teen who recently confided to his family that he is gay. "When Jay told us, my wife and I felt ashamed and hurt, which we understand now was not helpful to our son. After those feeings pass, you worry about the name-calling, which he says he's experiencing all the time. But then you think about AIDS.

"A counselor I talked to told me that it's really ironic, but that lots of gay teenagers ignore the danger, even feel as if they're sort of invulnerable. They don't know any other gay kids who have AIDS. They think it's for guys older than they are—twenties, thirties. But like this counselor says, it's foolish to think that, since it often takes up to ten years after contracting the disease before there are symptoms. In other words, these 'older' guys in their twenties and thirties, very likely got it when they were Jay's age."

MORE THAN STATISTICS

In *The Other America: Gay and Lesbian Youth*, four young people tell their own stories. Their stories, like their backgrounds, are very different from one another.

Tori, a city girl, has experienced a difficult childhood, as her mother was in and out of prison and rehabilitation for drug addiction and drug-related crimes. In junior high, Tori went through a rebellious time, skipping school and selling crack, a time, she says, when "I just don't know what I was thinking. I just felt bad all the time." Today, however, she is proud of herself and looks forward to a future with her current girlfriend.

Like Tori, Joe is a city kid who has endured a difficult childhood. He knew he was gay, he says, from the time he was four or five. Although his mother is supportive and he has a group of loyal friends, he says it makes him sad his father refuses to understand or support him.

Justin, a teen in his senior year of high school, comes from a sleepy little river town, miles from the city. He has recently come out, or admitted his homosexuality, to his mother, sister, and friends. His father and brother don't know, he says, although he thinks his father may have guessed. He is happy with his life, he says shyly, although he admits he experienced years of depression, feeling cut off from his peers and his family, most of whom "just assumed I was straight."

Finally, there is Nikki, a twenty-year-old university student who did not recognize that she was a lesbian until her senior year of high school. Although she says she did not suffer from depression and the feelings of isolation that burden many other young lesbians, she empathizes with the hurt that they feel. Planning a career of activism in the gay and lesbian community, she hopes she can make a difference.

Reading their accounts, straight readers will come away from these four young people with more of an understanding about what it feels like to be gay or lesbian in America today. For gay or lesbian readers, parts of the four stories may parallel their own experiences.

Tori

**"BEING A LESBIAN ISN'T JUST A
LITTLE PART OF MY PERSONALITY;
IT'S SOMETHING THAT'S
IMPORTANT TO ME, SOMETHING
THAT CAN'T REALLY BE
SEPARATED FROM HOW I THINK."**

Tori answers the door and opens it without smiling. She is small boned and petite, with close-cropped hair. She is dressed in baggy jeans, an old sweatshirt, and what look like new basketball high-tops.

"I play a lot of basketball," she says, with a hint of a smile. "I just got these last week, and I'm breaking them in."

The house is immaculate, with religious pictures and family portraits on every wall and tabletop. The shades are drawn in every room; the strong sunlight outside does not penetrate at all.

"This is my grandma's house," explains Tori. "I live here all the time. All the pictures, and the plants and everything, this is all hers.

"I guess she likes it kind of dark. But she spends all her time in bed nowadays; she's got some kind of upper respiratory disease. She has an inhaler, and she needs a machine to breathe sometimes.

"She even eats all her meals in bed. I don't know how she does that without getting heartburn or something. I try to get her to do things with me, to get out of the house once in a while, but she really doesn't like to. Only if she's got something important to do, like a doctor's appointment or something like that. But my grandpa is here, and my uncle on and off. So things get done. And she doesn't let her medical problems get her down much. She's really a mellow, relaxed, laid-back person."

A Scattered Family

Tori says that she has lived with her grandma most of her life, and she likes it that way.

"My mother and father never married," she says. "After they had me, they went their separate ways, I guess. My dad lives in Illinois now, and has nine other kids. And my mom has had two little boys since. My mom lives not too far from here, and I see her often; she stops in. But she can't have us there with her, because she's dealing with some things right now.

"Sometimes I get real upset with her, because she doesn't have me or my two brothers living all together with her. That's how we were once, but not for a long time. My one little brother lives here, and the other one lives south of here, with his father. Everybody is scattered.

"See, my mom got caught up in some trouble, doing crack and also getting in trouble for bad checks. We all were in Iowa for a while; she had a job. That was when I was young, but then the

Tori and her little brother Tyris are "very close," according to Tori. "He doesn't have a problem with my lesbianism. We always joke around and call each other names, but I know he doesn't mean any harm in it."

drugs got bad, and I went back here to live with my grandma. This feels like my home. Once my mom had us come to live with her for a little while, and I remember crying that I wanted to go back to my grandma's. It's more settled here."

Tori says that her mother is off drugs now, but she is uncertain whether her mother's condition is permanent.

"She's not on crack now, I know that," she says. "She's holding down a couple of jobs, trying to get on track. But she's been in and out of jails so often, and in and out of rehab, that it's clear that she has a history of slipping back sometimes. It upsets me. And like I said, my uncle is here, too. He was trying to get off drugs, but he's slipping back.

"I hate that, and I feel bad for my grandma. I mean, she didn't raise no kids so that they could grow up to be drug addicts. She brought them up right, but somehow they got messed up in it. I want to tell my uncle, 'Take that somewhere else; don't do it around here.' He's not trying to help himself—not at all."

"I'VE SORT OF KNOWN SINCE I WAS SIX OR SO"

Tori is a lesbian—a fact, she says, she has been aware of since she was a very small girl.

"I think I've always suspected," she says, carefully choosing her words. "Really I've sort of known since I was six or so. I remember that I used to fantasize dreams in my mind, kind of daydream the scenes. In these dreams, I'd be a guy, loving some girl. It was always something romantic. It never was like I was a superhero, or something like that—just me always with a girl, but being a guy.

"I never thought about those dreams then as being weird or different. I mean, who knows what people daydream about? For all I knew, everybody daydreamed stuff like that. Maybe it was just the way people were; what did I know? So I never compared myself to anyone else, never thought about it. It was just me, thinking about stuff during my quiet time."

But, says Tori, you find out when you get older that such thoughts are not considered normal by everyone's standards. Learning this can be a painful lesson.

"You hear those words when you get older," she says seriously. "You hear not only words like *lesbian* and *gay*, but you hear other words, too—*butch*, *dyke*, *fag*—stuff like that. And you know by the

15

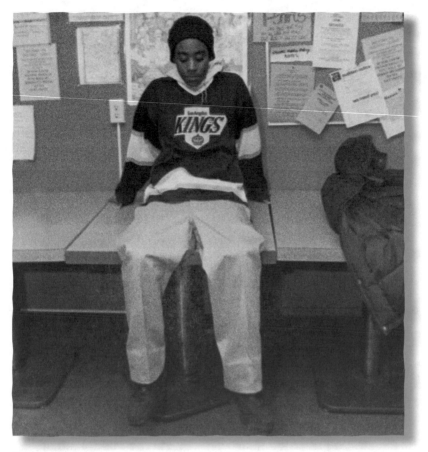

Tori admits that trying to keep a positive attitude about her sexuality has sometimes been difficult, especially when she hears people using derogatory words like dyke *and* butch *to refer to lesbians.*

way people say those words that they mean something bad. And then you learn what those words mean, and you realize that they are words about you, and then you get worried.

"I wondered, am I really bad? In some ways, it seemed somewhat positive to me, like on a physical level girls would hug girls, or whatever. That seemed okay. But when you'd hear the jokes at school, you'd think it was something bad, something you wouldn't want to admit."

BOYS WERE MORE FUN

Tori found boys far more interesting to be around than girls. However, some of the boys were as quick to tease her for her boyish haircut and clothing as some of the girls she knew.

"Boys were interesting," she says matter of factly. "I played sports a lot—basketball, volleyball, stuff like that. I'm pretty good, too. I mean, not to brag, but I am. I've played on teams, like at the Y, and I've done pretty well. And this one center for gay and lesbian kids is maybe going to get a team together for softball this spring. That would be lots of fun. I've never played softball, but I'm lucky in that I can usually pick up sports pretty fast.

"But even though I could hold my own with guys, some of them teased me, too. Even my friends, and that hurt a lot. They'd see me coming down the hall or something, and they'd say, 'What's up, dude?' See, I liked to dress in jeans and T-shirts and stuff. They talked to me like I was a guy and laugh. They were making fun of me because I dressed a certain way, maybe liked my hair shorter than some girls. I was tomboyish, but so what?

"When they'd do that, start laughing, I'd say, 'If you're supposed to be my friends, you wouldn't make fun of me. You'd

Playing pool at a gay and lesbian youth center is one of Tori's favorite pastimes. The only problem is the cramped space that makes it difficult to make a clear shot.

come and talk to me instead.' But it wasn't everybody. I mean, I had some friends that were girls that stuck up for me. I really *did* get a lot of stuff about my hair. Girls would say, 'Tori, why don't you put a perm in it or something?' But I'd always say that I liked it that way, that this is the way I am, so get used to it."

Giggling at Cheerleaders and Trying a Boyfriend

By the time she got to junior high, Tori's sexual feelings were becoming more intense. She was interested in girls, she said, but she had no way to act on those feelings.

"Back in fifth grade the closest I ever got was that me and my friend—a girl—used to stay after school and watch the cheerleaders," she says. "We'd go into the gym when there was a basketball game or something, and we'd look at the cheerleaders' breasts. We'd giggle and act stupid. I mean, after all, we were in fifth grade! I never told my friend how it made me feel, how it was kind of exciting. I don't think I said much of anything, really, and she didn't either. We were just immature, acting dumb.

"But later, when I was in junior high, things were different. I *knew* that what I was was a lesbian, and I also knew that people thought that was bad. So it was a rough time for me. I hadn't made any move to get involved with a girl, but I wanted to. But at the same time, I was getting lots of pressure to hang out, looking for boys. That was what girls did, I guess."

Tori says that her cousin was a real motivating factor in her search for boyfriends.

"She liked boys," says Tori, "but I was doing it kind of as a cover. I didn't want people to know how I felt about girls, so this was a perfect thing to do. So my cousin and I started hanging out, being what you call fast—staying out late, just looking for trouble. We'd lie about our age, too, telling guys that we were sixteen, when we were only thirteen.

"I did end up having lots of boyfriends, and that was stupid. There was one guy I especially liked. And we were seeing each other for like two months, and he kept pressuring me to have sex, to take the relationship to the next level. But with him, even though I really liked him, I didn't want to have sex. I was sort of curious what it would be like, but it felt very wrong when I thought about it.

"I almost did have sex with him," she admits. "It was mainly because I thought that if I did, he would stop pressuring me about it. Maybe he'd stop talking about it, right? But I couldn't. At the last minute, I backed out. And I couldn't be honest and tell him why. I wonder sometimes, even now, whether he would have understood if I'd told him about my feelings for girls. I just couldn't be open yet."

COMING OUT BY ACCIDENT

She had not told anyone yet about her sexual feelings, but that changed during her eighth-grade year. Her grandma was the first person to find out that she was a lesbian, and that was quite by accident.

"See, that year there was this woman named Tina who came to visit us from out of state. She was a friend of my aunt's, older than me. She was staying here at my grandma's. Anyway, I had met this woman before, and we got along real well. And so when she visited this time, she could sense that I was having these feelings. We talked a little about it.

Junior high school was frustrating for Tori, who concealed her sexual feelings at that time. "I knew that what I was was a lesbian, and I also knew that people thought that was bad," she recalls.

"I was fourteen, I think. My mom had a suspicion, I think, that something might be going on between me and Tina. She would say things like, 'Do you want to become like one of them?' She used some word like *dyke* or something mean like that.

"But we were seeing each other, and I enjoyed it. One time, my grandma was working late, and she came in and found us downstairs in bed. My grandma was so surprised, so shocked. She could hardly talk. Then she started yelling at Tina, saying, 'What are you doing in bed with my granddaughter?' She told her to get out right away, that she wouldn't have someone like her in the house.

"I was embarrassed and ran upstairs to the bathroom. My grandma was following me, saying, 'What are you doing? Are you a lesbian? Is that who you want to hang around with, lesbians?' I couldn't talk; I tried to just act cool, not argue."

TELLING STEPHANIE

Tori says that having her grandma find out about her sexual preference was scary but that the experience opened the door for her to come out to people she trusted.

"Stephanie was one person I felt like I could tell," says Tori. "I had an idea that she could be a lesbian, too, but I wasn't really sure. She'd never come out to me or anything, but it was just a feeling that I had, from how she talked. Even if she wasn't a lesbian, though, I knew she would try to be understanding and supportive.

"I remember calling her on the phone one night. I was lying on the bed, being real nervous about bringing it up. I mean, I wanted to, but I was starting to get cold feet, you know? I told her that there was something important that I had to tell her. She's like, 'Tori, what is it?' She sounded really worried.

"I didn't know how to say it. I just kept stalling and evading it. Then finally I blurted it out, and she says, 'That's *it*? That's the big news?' I told her yeah, that I didn't know how she'd feel. Maybe she wouldn't want to be friends with a lesbian, I said. But she laughed, and we talked about it. No big deal. She wasn't surprised at all."

That episode had an ironic ending, says Tori with a smile. Stephanie told her she was interested in her romantically.

Tori talks to a friend from her grandmother's house, where she has lived for most of her life.

WRITING A LETTER

How about others in her family? Did she finally let them know? Tori smiles sheepishly.

"A couple of years ago I wrote a letter to my mom. I know it sounds cowardly, but I just couldn't face her if she cried or made a scene. I left the letter on the bed; I knew she was due to come over. I told my grandma that I was going away for the weekend, and I left.

"The note was sort of to the point, I guess. I explained how it was for me, all the things I felt. I'd been thinking about telling her for a while, but the time was never right. So this seemed the best way.

"As it turned out, the letter worked okay. She found out where I was staying that weekend, and she called me. She told me that I didn't have to leave, that we could have talked about it, the two of us. That made me feel better. So I came back, and we did talk. She didn't act very surprised, because of what had happened before, when she suspected Tina and me of seeing each other."

What about her father?

"No," she says simply. "Why should I? He's never taken any responsibility on his part to see how I'm doing, how I'm growing
up. So if I talked to him, all this frustration I feel would come out.
But I did talk to my god-dad, though. I was scared to tell him, because he's Muslim and has real strict ideas about right and wrong.
But he's also a counselor, and so I thought he might be able to
deal with it pretty good.

"He turned out to be understanding, and that was a relief. We
had gone out for dinner one time, and he said, 'Your mom tells me
you're having some problems.' I didn't say anything: I didn't know
what I should say. And so then he tells me that anytime I have a

*Tori realized that she was a lesbian when she was six years old. Her family is
very accepting of her sexuality. "I wish we could talk more about it, but we
don't. Maybe that's because I don't talk about it. When I do bring girlfriends
home, they get a good reception, though."*

problem I could come and talk to him. That was really nice. I trust him. Plus, he works not that far from here, so I get to see him a lot."

GETTING INTO TROUBLE

Besides coming to terms with her sexuality during her years in junior high, Tori says that she was dealing with other matters, which today seem to be embarrassing to talk about.

"I got in a lot of trouble during eighth and ninth grade," she admits. "I don't think it had anything to do with my sexuality except maybe in the sense that I was going through a lot of rebellion and stress at that time. My grades had been pretty good up until the end of eighth grade, but they started really sliding. And by ninth grade, I sort of lost it. And because my grades were so bad, I was ineligible for basketball and stuff—and that was hard on me. The sports were the number one thing I enjoyed, and without them, school was boring. I stopped trying.

"See, I was arrested for selling drugs. I mean there were a couple other things I got in trouble for, like skipping school, or driving a car without a license, stuff like that. And I'd got caught with drugs that time I was driving—it was real late at night, and I got nailed. I went to juvenile detention—I think just for a weekend or something. But I got me a probation officer, and he was pretty cool. I just went off to some group home for a couple of days, and then I left. That was pretty much it.

"I really got in trouble. See, I had been selling drugs—mostly crack—for a while. And I *know*, I *know*, it was a dumb thing to do, especially with my mom and my uncle doing those drugs and everything. At least I wasn't using the drugs, just selling. But it was a dumb thing to do. I don't know what I was thinking of back then."

Tori says that either she and a friend bought and sold a large quantity of drugs together, or she did it alone, getting the drugs from a dealer and splitting the profits with him.

"Either way, it wasn't hard to get rid of them," she says. "I sold to anyone, anywhere I could. A lot of the time I'd go to a part of the city that was a heavy drug area and either be on some corner or else use a house where lots of people congregated.

"Anyway, this time I was with a friend of mine. We'd taken a taxi into a big drug area. I got out, walked about three blocks, and then the cops pulled me over. They asked me if I had drugs on me, and I said no at first. I told them I wasn't carrying anything, that I was just walking to the bus station. But of course, I had drugs in my mouth, in little plastic bags, and I had about five hundred dollars' worth stuck in my bra.

"But they didn't believe me; I could tell that right away. Now, I could have gotten away with this. I could have swallowed the stuff in my mouth, and they'd never have searched the rest of me—at least, not right away. But I didn't.

"The cops grabbed my neck and I spit the stuff out. I really don't know how they knew I was carrying, since I had been doing this long enough to have gotten used to talking real plain with the stuff jammed up above my gums. You get so you don't mumble or anything. But somehow they knew, I guess."

Tori says that the result of her crime was that she was sent to the northern part of the state to a work camp for girls who were chronic offenders.

"I didn't mind it at all, really," she claims. "Other than the fact that I was doing time, it could have been a vacation. I know lots of the girls there didn't like it, but to me it was sort of woodsy, like camping. I didn't mind being far from civilization. Nothing was easy; we still had to go to school and do some physical work. But I'm not afraid of that stuff—I could handle it pretty easy."

BACK TO CIVILIZATION

Her return from the work camp to school was not easy. Tori says that she had lost interest in school, although she tried to keep up with her assignments.

"My being lesbian wasn't really an issue anymore, at least for most people," she says. "I wasn't real open about it; only a few close friends knew. But I think people just sort of figured it out. They knew without me telling them, you know?

"Some people would even say, 'Tori, I've been hearing stuff about you being lesbian.' I'd ask them, 'So if I am, is there a problem with that?' Usually that kind of ended the discussion. Either they accepted me, or they didn't. Part of me really didn't care all that much, because school was less important.

"Part of the problem for me coming back was the way my school was run," she says. "Nothing seemed too important, and the principal was really clear about the fact that he didn't like me or trust me. I felt like he'd singled me out, probably because he

24

Tori hangs out at a center for gay and lesbian youth to socialize, to get information about things that are going on, and to use the computers.

knew about the trouble I'd been in and that I'd been sent up north. But the reality of the situation was that I was not selling drugs anymore, not at all.

"But he kept up the pressure on me. For a while, he was mad at me for wearing a head wrap. I always did; it was part of who I was. But he kept insisting that I had to take it off. I wouldn't. I told him it was religious, like a symbol of my African-American culture. I even had a guy I knew from the Inner City Youth League come in and talk to the principal, explain about it. But no way—that man was too stubborn.

"The last straw for me was an incident that happened at school, where marijuana was being smoked. I was nearby when it was happening, but I had nothing to do with it. I didn't sell the marijuana, I didn't use it—nothing. It was two guys who were smoking it, I guess. And the principal decided to detain me, because I wasn't denying anything. I mean, lots of the other people were being real defensive, saying, 'I didn't do anything, I had nothing to do with it.' But not me. I knew I was innocent, so I refused to go through the little dance for the principal.

"I was mad, especially when he let the two guys who were smoking it go and tells me he's going to search my bag and have a male police officer search me. I'm like, 'No, you're *not* going to have anybody search me. I was so angry that I called my mom. I was crying. The whole thing was so unfair, so wrong of him. It got straightened out later, but the whole thing left me so angry at the school and that principal, that I changed to another school.

"This place I'm in now is less structured. You have a little more time to explore ideas and stuff. It's a school for the arts, sort of run at your own pace. I've just started there, so I'm just starting to figure out what's possible. I know the math teacher is cool. You get a credit after you finish twenty math work sheets. I guess I can handle that easy enough."

KARISA

Today, Tori is more calm than she has been for the last two or three years. A large part of that, she says, is that she has a girlfriend about whom she cares deeply.

"Her name is Karisa," says Tori with a smile. "She's white, with short blond hair, and a fantastic personality. We met in a gay bar after one in the morning, when they weren't carding people. She remembers seeing me in the bathroom first, but I don't remember that. We got together on the dance floor and really had fun. After that she asked if me and my friend would like to meet her and her friend at an open-all-night place near there.

"Well, we did, and we got to talking, and things kind of went on from there. We got to know each other, talking on the phone all the time, and she liked me real well. So we've been hitting it off ever since. We've been going together for a little over six months now.

"Our first date was supposed to be the state fair, but we didn't get around to doing that. We go to movies, talk on the phone, just hang out a lot. She's a lot older than me—she's twenty-two—but we seem to have a lot of things in common."

Tori says that Karisa has also been a motivating force in getting her to attend school and get her grades up.

"She's in college, not too far from here," she explains. "And she's a real good student, has lots of self-motivation. She is not the kind of person who needs a teacher or parent or someone telling her to finish a project or do homework. She just does it and usu-

Tori credits her girlfriend Karisa (background) with inspiring her to do well in school.

ally doesn't mind it at all. Anyway, Karisa gets me going, gets me excited about being successful at school. I've been reading lots, and I never have been a reader before.

"Sure, there are things we don't share, like a love for eighties music. I absolutely hate it, but Karisa is really into it. I just laugh at her. And we argue about really controversial subjects, like religion and politics. I mean, I have a tendency to get all emotional and run off at the mouth when I'm arguing. But Karisa will stop me and tell me to read something so I know more facts. That way the argument can mean something."

PLANS

Tori is unfazed by questions about her future. She says she has many dreams, but many of them involve getting into the politics of the gay and lesbian community.

"I went to a conference recently for gay and lesbian youth," she says. "I was really struck by how few minorities were represented.

Tori and her brother Tyris perform a rap that Tori wrote for a Black History Month celebration.

I'd like to get involved, maybe start something of my own. This being a lesbian isn't just a little part of my personality; it's something that's important to me, something that can't really be separated from how I think.

"Karisa's been helping me find materials and stuff that would be good for me to have. She's been looking with me through some college catalogs, maybe to find some courses I might take someday to get more informed, you know?

"I'm spending a lot of time working at the center I mentioned before—for gay and lesbian teens. I enjoy it, but there are problems there. For one thing, I was so surprised to find how often I get harassed down there, more than I did at school! I mean, of all places you think would be safe, I'd have put the center at the top of the list.

"It's mainly the queens, the guys who are really effeminate, who dress up sometimes, and call themselves by women's names. They'll say to me, 'Oh, you're so fine, you're so cute, can I touch you here?' That really makes me mad. I told the director of the center, and she said she'd keep an eye on that. So the next time, not too long after I reported it, it happened again.

"I told them, 'Leave me alone. Why is it every time I come here I get harassed by some guy?' And I said to the director, 'You see that, don't you?' She told this one queen, the one who kind of starts it, 'Celeste, that can't be happening anymore.' But it will again, I'm sure. And that's bad for us as a community. We need to stick together, to be supportive of one another, not doing that stuff that Celeste and them are doing."

One thing that Tori has tried to do at the center is get involved in the planning of activities, often with Karisa's advice or encouragement.

"I am really working hard, organizing a program for Black History Month at the center," she says. "I'm doing lots of reading, learning things I never knew before, stuff I never heard in school. It feels so much more worthwhile to me, learning about that kind of thing, than all the junk we were doing in school sometimes. And maybe, I'm thinking, maybe this will kind of have an effect on the kids at the center; maybe they'll think more about things if they can learn a little. Maybe the community will get along better . . . I don't know."

STAYING WITH KARISA

While Tori seems very hopeful that the relationship between her and Karisa can last, she is unsure about the particulars of the arrangement.

"I kind of want to move out of my grandma's next summer," she says. "I kind of think it's time. And right now Karisa is in a place she shares with a roommate. We've talked about maybe moving in together this summer. I'd like that a lot.

"But the one thing is that she'll be graduating from college next year. She's thinking maybe she'd like to go to San Francisco. I want to come to, but I don't know. I guess I haven't thought about that much. Hopefully, I mean, if I had my way, we would stay around here for a while. That's a big step, you know, moving so far away. I think I'd like to see how it goes, just living together for a while."

Tori says that she might someday want children, although she and Karisa haven't decided anything.

"I think about it," she says. "But really, it depends on where I'm at. I want to do something, to contribute something. Even if it's not a big deal, like being some kind of advocate, even if it's just finding a place to open a coffee shop or a bookstore, or something. Somewhere that people can relax, talk. But I've got to have some stability to think about kids. If my life isn't real stable, it wouldn't be fair to bring kids into my life, would it?"

"IT'S HARDER BEING LESBIAN THAN STRAIGHT"

The lifestyle Tori has is perhaps not what she would have chosen for herself, if she'd had a choice.

"It's harder being lesbian than straight," she says slowly, thinking about her choice of words. "But I don't want to make it sound like I don't like who I am. It's just like saying it's easier for white people than black people, but that doesn't mean I wish I were white. I don't. But I'm glad I am who I am. It's like saying, 'I wish I had blue eyes,' or 'Why can't I be taller?'

"I'm proud of who I am, of the kind of person I'm becoming. I've made mistakes, but I've gotten over them. I will still keep making them, but hopefully not the same ones. I mean, everybody is human; we all mess up sometimes.

"But it *is* a harder lifestyle for gays and lesbians, especially young people. Just approaching people is hard. I mean, at the center, you pretty much know that any girl in there is either lesbian or bisexual, so it's not as risky. Some of the girlfriends I've had have come from there. But that's such a small world. You're always talking to someone who has gone out with your friend, or whatever. It gets too close, you know? Plus, just going there and being harassed, it's not always fun.

"So what do you do when you're in the mall, or just out on the streets? There, people aren't all lesbian and gay. And how do you know?"

Tori says that it is very difficult for her to approach girls she doesn't know are straight or lesbian.

When she was younger, Tori hung around boys more than girls. Although they teased her about her clothes and short haircut, the boys were more fun.

"Heterosexuals can approach anybody they want," she shrugs. "If they get rejected, they don't need to take it personally or worry they've offended someone. If the other person turns them down, it wasn't a personal judgment against them.

"But like me, if I try talking to another girl and she turns out to be straight, she takes it real personally. She gets offended that she might have given out the wrong signal somehow, like there's some defect in her personality. She gets all freaked out, and then I feel bad, too. But when you think about it, isn't it sort of a compliment if someone thinks you're attractive, whether that person is lesbian or straight? It's just someone who doesn't know you, saying that you look interesting, worth getting to know. It shouldn't be a big deal, really."

"IT'S NO GOOD KEEPING SECRETS"

If she were asked by a younger girl—perhaps thirteen or fourteen—who is sure she is a lesbian or who is having questions about her sexuality, Tori says there is some definite advice she would offer.

"For one thing," she begins, "you got to be ready to talk to people. Whether it's a counselor at your school or someone you feel you can trust without them spreading it around, that's what you've got to do. I mean, even if you can tell a friend, or even one of your parents, that's a start.

"It's no good keeping secrets, though. You've got to tell someone. And if you get really stranded, you can call a helpline or something. I know lots of people who have used them, including me. When I came back from the camp up north, I called a helpline, because I wanted to make a start, I wanted to find a school where there were programs or support groups for gay and lesbian kids.

"They were real helpful, too, real understanding. They told me about the center, where I've met lots of people And they gave me a list of programs, a list of places I could call to get information on places to go to meet kids. Then you're kind of set, you know? I've even gotten hooked up with a couple of mentors—older people you can really trust if you need some help, advice about your future, or even just want to talk. One of my mentors was a professor at the university, and that was cool."

Whatever someone chooses to do, says Tori, it's important to know that you're not alone. There are plenty of other kids in your community, in your city, that are going through the same ordeals, trying to deal with the same issues.

"You just have to get organized," she says. "The way I did it was have a notebook, where I keep a lot of phone numbers of people and organizations that can help. I mean, there are lots of resources out there for kids to use, and they don't cost anything. You may not need them today or even this year. But they might come in handy someday. Who knows?"

Joe

"I THINK KIDS ARE BETTER OFF GETTING THEIR STRENGTH FROM INSIDE THEMSELVES. IF I COULD THINK OF SOMETHING TO TELL KIDS THAT ARE STRUGGLING WITH THE REALIZATION THAT THEY'RE GAY, I'D SAY THEY SHOULD FIND OUT ALL THEY CAN ABOUT IT."

His smile is wide, lighting up his delicate features. He is small boned and slight, built like a gymnast. He is sixteen and of mixed race—African American and white. He goes by the name of Joe, he says, because he hates his real name.

"It's Jewuan," he says, crinkling up his nose in disgust. "It's French, from the root name Jeremiah. I found that out just the other day. I was at the mall, and they have these places you can go and get a printout of your name and the story of it or something. And that's mine. Anyway, Joe is much better!"

"I DON'T LIVE AT HOME"

Joe lives in the city, a few blocks from the interstate.

"It's not my real home," he explains. "It's a foster care place. I'm living with two gay men who are going to be my guardians. I'm gay, and I guess it made sense to try to get into a group home where the adults are gay, too. I guess I feel more comfortable, not having to explain myself, or be hassled with questions all the time.

"I don't live at home. Before I moved in with these guys, I was living in a shelter. I wasn't put there; I put myself there. My mother and I don't see eye to eye right now.

"Not that it has anything to do with my sexuality," he is quick to add. "I mean, she knows I'm gay, and she's totally fine with it. It's just the same stuff that's been going on for years."

Joe draws a deep breath.

"My mom does drugs, see, and I don't like that," he says. "She lives with my stepfather, Stefan. At least, she did until he got arrested for molesting two girls. And I have three sisters: Tineka, who is nine, Ashley, who is four, and the baby, Amber. She's about five and a half months now.

"Before that, when I was ten, Stefan went to jail for assaulting someone," Joe says, rolling his eyes in disgust. "He's really a great guy, huh? I mean, just the kind of person, just the kind of home you want to grow up in. He was gone for like two or three years. But *please* make sure it's clear that I'm not related to him. My sisters are, but not me."

A FAMILY SPLIT APART

Joe says that his family has been splintered because of his stepfather's abuse and by his mother's drug use. When Joe was eleven, his mother was arrested in a drug raid. It was even more traumatic because he and his sister were present when it happened.

"I remember my sister, Tineka, and I were there that night at my mom's friend's house, and we were getting really sleepy—it was at night. We kept telling my mom we wanted to go home. We were only like six blocks from home, but it was snowing like crazy, so my mom called a cab.

"Me and my sister were waiting in the back room, getting sleepier by the minute waiting for that cab. It took so long, I guess, because of the blizzard outside. Anyway, the grownups were doing crack and stuff like that, when all of a sudden, we hear this big commotion coming from the front room.

"All of a sudden, BAM! Somebody kicks the door in in the bedroom where me and my sister was, and like five policemen came in, pointing guns at us. We started crying, we were so scared. What if they thought I was some big-time drug user and they started shooting me, or the gun went off before they knew I was just a kid?"

Joe says his most vivid memory of that night was seeing his mother and his aunt, along with the other adults, being led out in handcuffs.

35

Joe has spent most of his life separated from his siblings. One of the reasons he came back to live at his mother's house was because of his sister Amber (pictured); however, he could not tolerate his mom's drug use and left again.

"It was so weird," he says. "They put towels over everyone's heads so we couldn't see their faces. They threw them down on the floor to put the cuffs on them, just like on television. Even with the towels, I knew which one was my aunt, because of what she was wearing. And my mom . . . well, I just knew her."

Following that incident, Joe and his sister were removed from their mother's care.

"We went to a shelter and after that went to foster care for about a year," he says. "Tineka got real sick with a really high fever when we got to the shelter, and had to go in the hospital. By the time she was well again and came back to the shelter, I had been placed in a foster home. They were supposed to not split us up, but since we have different last names, they didn't know we were brother and sister. The bureaucracy just screwed up."

"It Wasn't Always Bad"

Joe pauses, as if he is dissatisfied with the way his story is going.

"I don't want to make my mom out to be a really bad person," he says. "I mean, lots of this is my stepfather's fault. My mom wasn't always on crack, and when she's off the drugs, she's a really normal-seeming person. You'd never guess it.

"She graduated high school, straight-A student, and went to college. She quit school after a couple of years because she and my dad had gotten together, and she had me. But she was planning to go back, planning to be a social worker I think. She had her life straight, you know; she knew what she was doing back then. And after I was born, she was just getting her life back in order, was planning to return to college, when she met Stefan. That was the start of the problems.

"They met when we were living in Chicago and then had my sister after that. I was six then, I think. At first Stefan was really nice to me. He got me a little golden retriever puppy for my birthday. I was really excited, because I'd never had any kind of pet before. Then we moved back here and stayed for a while in this big old house with my aunt.

"But then he and my aunt got in a big fight about something. He drew a gun on her, and she threw a lamp down the stairs at him. I'm pretty sure he was on drugs then, but I know my mom wasn't.

"I was happy until then, I think. The first bad thing was getting kicked out of my aunt's house. Then we moved into this really shitty apartment. And my puppy? He mysteriously 'ran away.' At least that's what I was told then. I don't believe that now, and I never did—I think he killed the dog. Years later he was mad at me and kind of jeered at me that he had buried my puppy in the backyard. God, that made me feel so bad when he said that."

ABUSE

Joe's voice gets very quiet.

"I guess the worst part of that time was that he started abusing my mom, especially after she had Ashley. He'd hit her, choke her. I remember when I was eight or nine and my sister was only two, he choked my mom. . . . He was hitting her, and had his hands around her neck. She was screaming for me to call the police. And he was screaming at me, telling me that if I did that, he'd kill me.

"So anyway, she passed out. It was so weird; one minute she was screaming really loud, and the next minute, she wasn't. Then my stepfather walked up to me and told me to call the police. He must have changed his mind, though, because as soon as I dialed 911, he grabbed the phone away and told the operator that I was just playing.

"And so I went back where she was lying, and I looked at her. She had bruises all over her neck. She didn't wake up even when I shook her. I was afraid she was dead. He took off running out the door. Then I called the police, and they came and took care of her."

Joe says many of his family's problems can be traced to his stepfather Stefan's abuse. Stefan would often taunt Joe about his lack of masculinity.

Joe shakes his head.

"It was so stupid, when I think back on it now. I mean, he comes back like a week later, and nothing happened to him! She wouldn't press charges against him, so it just kept going like that, him being abusive and her getting hurt, and him never having to face up to what he did. This happened all through their marriage."

"I FELT LIKE I SHOULD BE ASHAMED"

Joe says that in addition to thinking a lot about his mother and his stepfather's abuse, he wondered about being different from other kids his age.

"It's really hard to explain," he says, "because I didn't ever play outside with other kids. Honest. I think I was twelve before I actually got out just to fool around. My mom sheltered us, and because of the neighborhoods we lived in, she didn't want us to mix with the kids who lived nearby. I didn't want to, either. I was kind of shy, and it wasn't easy for me to approach someone and start a conversation.

"Anyway, I played a lot by myself inside. I know now that the toys and things I liked maybe pointed to me being gay, but back then I didn't have a word for it or anything. I liked Barbies. I played with them as often as GI Joes and Kung Fu fighters. And I really liked playing in one of my mom's old nighties.

"My absolute hero back then was Wonder Woman. I had Wonder Woman glasses, and a painting smock with Wonder Woman on it. I would wrap a towel around my head and spin around, and my hair came down like Wonder Woman's did. She was so cool.

"My mom never said much about it. She says now that she always kind of thought I might be gay. But it didn't completely freak her out the way it did Stefan. When he came to live with us, he got me started feeling like what I was doing was not only different, but weird and very wrong. I remember. I felt like I should be ashamed.

"Stefan would take any feminine clothes I had, like that old nightie of my mom's, and toys that were 'girl' toys; he'd take them away. Once he burned a bunch of stuff that he didn't think was right for me to have. Then he sat me down and tried to explain to me about being a man, how what I was doing was really stupid and wrong. He'd tried to get me into doing stuff with the boys in the neighborhood, like basketball or stuff like that. Basketball was his thing, but I wasn't interested in sports."

39

Joe thinks for a moment, as if sorting it out in his head first.

"See, it was like to him if I wasn't doing something like that, I was someone weird—a freak or something. He was trying to save me. What I mostly hated was when we'd be out somewhere, and he would be pointing out these girls. He'd say, 'Do you think she's cute?' or 'Do you like that one?' I mean, I was six or seven, and he'd be doing that. He still does it. I just play along, just say, 'Yeah, yeah she is.' I wanted him to shut up, and that was the only way."

Joe says that his mother would sometimes try to stick up for her son, but usually to no avail.

"She'd tell him to lay off, to leave me alone," he says. "But that could start a fight, and I didn't want her getting hit on account of that stuff. Or sometimes, she wasn't around, and he'd just keep it up, keep it up."

BACK AND FORTH

A year after Joe and Tineka were taken away, he was placed back in his mother's home. Tineka remained in the care system, spending time in shelters, foster homes, and even in the care of relatives.

"My mom was off the drugs," says Joe, "and she seemed to be back on track. Stefan was in jail for assaulting someone, so it was a little more relaxing at home. My mom was pregnant with Ashley, ready to deliver any time.

"The weekend before she had my sister, we had quite a scare. We were in this shopping center, and she said something to me. I turned around to see what she wanted, and she was looking at me kind of funny. Then she lets go of the shopping cart, and falls back. The sound was awful—just this loud, echoing crack. I run over to her, and there's a pool of blood by her head. She started shaking, having a seizure. She'd just passed out."

Was it drugs again? Joe isn't sure.

"I don't think so. I mean, they took her to the hospital, and if she'd had crack in her blood, you'd think they'd find it. Or maybe she'd been drinking. I don't know. I think maybe she was hungry and tired. But then a couple days later, she had Ashley, and that was cool. But then she relapsed, when Ashley was still a little baby, only a month old. And what happened then still makes me furious, even though it was four years ago. It just shows you how you can't trust the stupid bureaucracy.

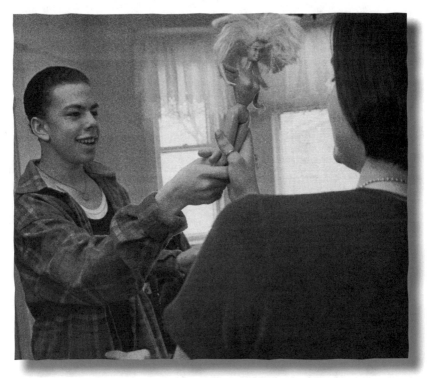

Joe goofs around during a visit to his friend Cinta's house. When Joe was younger, he liked playing with Barbies. He also dressed up and imitated his heroine, Wonder Woman.

"She went to her social worker or whatever, and told her that she had relapsed. She needed some help getting clean again, and she knew she also had to find a new place to live. See, that was the biggest thing. We were in transitional housing, and when you relapse, they kick you out.

"This is what makes me mad. They told her to put me and Ashley in a shelter for a couple of days, to give her time to find an apartment, and to get started on rehab. Then we would be returned to her. A couple of days, that was all. I mean, she went to them, she was honest, she told them what was happening, and was asking for help.

"But what did they do? When my mom found a place and got herself started in a new drug program, she went to get us, but they told her to forget it. They wouldn't let us go back. That was the last time I saw my sister Ashley for a year and a half. For us, it was being bounced around from shelter to foster care, then to more shelters."

A Difficult Time

Joe says that his years going from shelter to foster home were difficult at first.

"I missed my mom," he admits. "At first all I thought about was going back. I told myself I didn't really care if she used drugs or drank or whatever. I used to defend her if anybody said anything against her.

"And another bad thing was not being able to tell anyone where I lived. I didn't really have my own home, my own address. Half the times when I'd be filling out forms or whatever for school, I couldn't even remember where I was living that month.

"I remember seventh grade was a really sad time for me—not school, but just that age. It may be that I was still coming to grips with my feelings toward some other boys, although I had not mentioned a word of my sexuality to anyone. I was starting to wonder, though, if I would ever find someone to go out with, someone I liked. So that—plus being worried about my mom, thinking about my life going by and nothing good happening—

Joe has spent most of his life living in shelters and foster homes. The instability of these homes, coupled with the anxiety Joe was feeling about his homosexuality and future, caused him to contemplate suicide.

I thought a lot about killing myself. I didn't try, but I sure thought about it a lot."

Joe says that he continued to be shy, and that probably made his situation more difficult.

"Making friends was still hard for me. At the shelters it was the worst. I mean, some were okay, but a lot of them I really hated. The one thing that was especially hard was that most of the other kids in these places had real problems. They'd been sent to shelters or put in foster homes because of stuff they'd done. One kid had hit his dad on the head with a baseball bat! Criminals, most of them were. And I was there for something else—supposedly because I was being protected!"

FACE TO FACE

One of the most remarkable things that happened during his time away from his mother was that he was reunited with his real father for a brief, uncomfortable time.

"They couldn't find a foster home for me," he explains, his face drawn and tense. "They didn't have anywhere else to put me, because they only let you stay in a particular group home for so long. So they just told me that I was going to live with my dad, in a little town southeast of here.

"I'd met him once or twice back in kindergarten. But now I was twelve, and I was really upset when they told me I was going with him. I'm like, 'What?' He'd never tried to keep up a relationship with me, so I had no great feelings toward him. I knew some stuff about him, though. I know he used to be big-time into drugs. But then he became a Jehovah's Witness, and all of a sudden he was too good for everybody."

Joe laughs bitterly.

"He acted like my mom was a piece of shit, like he was way above her now that he'd found religion. But just two years before, he'd been the same piece of shit, you know? It was so hypocritical it made me sick.

"So anyway, now I'm twelve, and he's bringing me to his house. He's saying things like, 'Well, well, we've got to buy you a suit.' I asked him why, and he tells me he's getting married. Nice way to find out, you know? So I was mad, because the group home didn't consult me, didn't ask me if it was okay with me to go with my father. After all, I was twelve, and I wasn't a baby."

The only good part of that time, says Joe, is that his new step-mother turned out to be very nice.

"They're getting a divorce now, so you know she's got some sense," he smiles. "I really love her. I sometimes go down there and just visit her. She lives like two blocks from him, so if I'm careful, I can avoid him altogether. I think of her as another mom. So in a way, I'm glad I spent that time down there. Getting to know her was worth it."

SURVIVING

On the other hand, he found school less of a struggle than his time at foster homes or shelters.

"I just was quiet," he says with a smile. "I tried to stay in the background all the time. This was sort of in junior high, I guess. Maybe there were people that teased me for that, but I don't re-member it. I didn't have any friends, but I didn't feel like I had en-emies, either. In my whole eighth grade, I was voted most quiet and best reader. I guess because that's all anyone ever saw me do."

Looking back, Joe says, he was able to survive most of that time by keeping a unique perspective on things.

"Like I said, sometimes I was really depressed, but mostly I tried to remove myself from what was going on," he says with a shrug. "It's hard to understand, maybe. But like, one time not too long ago, my aunt was talking to me, and she said, 'Jewuan, you've been through a lot. If I'd gone through all that when I was young, I'd have cracked.'

"So I guess to keep from cracking up, from going crazy, I tried to look on all of this stuff like it was a big adventure. Going from place to place was an adventure. Struggling with my sexuality and what that meant was an adventure. I tried not to think about it, tried not to talk about it to anyone. That was better for me, and it sort of kept me sane."

"I'M TWICE AS OLD AS I REALLY AM"

Another reason Joe thinks that he was able to cope with his diffi-cult childhood is that he has always been self-reliant.

"Like I said before, I'm used to being on my own, used to mak-ing decisions," he says. "I've always been kind of a little adult, be-cause my mom wasn't in charge, you know? I was the one who fed the girls, who cleaned things up and looked after everyone.

"It was a lot of responsibility, and I won't lie and say that I liked being in charge. Sometimes it made me really sad, that I was missing doing kid things. Like, for example, my mom always told me not to open the door when I was baby-sitting my sisters. Legally, I wasn't really old enough back when I was a little boy to be home with those girls alone. I had to keep the door closed.

"So one afternoon, my aunt comes to the door yelling, 'Jewuan, Jewuan, I know you're in there. Come on out, boy, I'm going to take you to the amusement park.' Oh, man, I wanted to open that door so bad. I mean, I'd never been to that amusement park, and

Joe has had to rely on himself, rather than an adult, during his short life. "I've always been kind of a little adult, because my mom wasn't in charge, you know?"

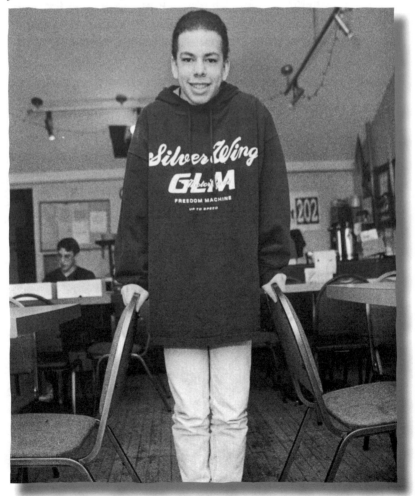

I'd always wanted to go. But I didn't open the door, because it would have made my mom really mad. So it didn't happen."

Joe leans back in his chair and gets philosophical.

"I feel right now like I'm in my thirties, not sixteen," he says seriously. "I know that seems funny. But it's true. In my mind, I'm twice as old as I really am."

TROUBLE AGAIN

Once he was in ninth grade, Joe says, his days at school were no longer tolerable.

"I was going to this high school, and I absolutely hated it," he says. "I don't really know why, because a lot of the kids were familiar to me; they'd gone to the same junior high. But I didn't want to be around them in ninth grade. I can't explain it. I'm sure it had something to do with being gay and wanting to start exploring what that meant for me, but I really don't know. All I knew was that I had to get out of that school, because I just couldn't take it anymore—and I didn't know what 'it' was!

High school was awkward for Joe; he wanted to start exploring his sexuality but felt inhibited by his fellow students.

"The way I handled it was really bizarre for me," he says with more than a little embarrassment. "I started hanging around with these really bad kids, kids I'd never have associated with before. We'd skip school, steal cars. I got caught, spent time in juvenile detention, then in a group home for kids that were troublemakers."

It was at this group home, says Joe, that he started being teased and called names by some of the other boys.

"They called me faggot and stuff like that," he says, shrugging. "I don't know why they were doing that, because no one had ever done that before. I'd never said anything about being gay. But I was still quiet and never talked about having a girlfriend, which most of them did.

"And one night, when I was sleeping, I woke up suddenly. There were some kids that had been putting Tabasco sauce on my lips while I was sleeping so that I would lick it. Then just before they ran out of my room, they poured a whole bunch down my throat.

"There were a lot of kids running out of my room, but I couldn't identify them," he says. "I was choking and couldn't catch my breath. I felt really sad about it, that they would do that to me without even knowing me. So I told some of the staff what had happened, but they didn't do anything about it. So at that point, I decided, I'm running away."

AN ACCIDENT

To make his getaway, Joe went to school and stole a car. He ended up getting into an accident, however, and narrowly escaped being seriously injured.

"It was so stupid," he says. "I'm driving pretty fast, and all of a sudden, the street just turned. But I didn't, since there was no sign to warn me. There was a tree up ahead, and I was just in a trance, watching it get closer and closer. Now I wonder sometimes if I maybe wanted to run into the tree.

"I don't know. I swerved, slammed into a parked car at forty-five miles an hour. I bashed my head into the steering wheel, but I was basically fine. The result was that I was arrested and sent to detention for a month. After that, another group home, this time way out in the boondocks."

He had more trouble fitting in there, he says, because he was of mixed race, and kids that far from the city were suspicious of him.

"I had no friends, and yet I found myself having fantasies about some of the boys there," he admits. "I never made any kind of a move toward them, though, because I'm sure they weren't gay. But I spent a lot of time thinking about other guys. I know I was feeling trapped in a situation where there was no way I could become a sexual person. All of a sudden, I was thinking of myself, 'Okay, you're gay.' But okay, fine, I'm gay, but *now* what do I do?"

COMING OUT, GRADUALLY

What Joe did was to sit down with his social worker and discuss the issue with him.

"It started a whole chain of events," says Joe. "When I told my social worker, he told the lady in charge of the group home. And she told my other worker. The result was that I got placed in a gay foster home. Not the one I'm in now, but just as nice. It opened up a whole new world for me, in terms of being gay.

"I didn't know exactly what I expected at that foster home. But they were just like normal people, just normal people. I moved in on July 1, and two weeks later there was a gay pride celebration not far from where we lived, so we all went.

"It was amazing! I think that was the first time I understood what being gay was all about. I mean, when you're little you hear so much wrong information about homosexuality, it takes a while to sort out the bull from the truth.

"Like, I remember when I was real young hearing that gay people were guys who acted like women because they secretly wanted to be women. And when I was young, and Stefan used to lecture me on how weird I was, I was sure that being gay didn't really apply to me, since I had no wish to be a woman, you know?

"But hearing the people speaking at that gay pride celebration was really cool. There were lots and lots of men who had made the decision to come out to their family, their friends, their co-workers. It seemed brave, but it made sense, too. I didn't think I was ready to tell the world, but I had to admit it was something I started really thinking about."

THE PARTY

When it came time to go back to school in the fall, Joe decided to switch to another high school, one that had an excellent support system for gay and lesbian teens.

Coming out was a gradual process for Joe. With the help of a social worker, he was placed in a gay foster home that he says "opened up a whole new world for me, in terms of being gay."

"It was amazing," Joe says. "It changed my life. I mean, for the first time, I had a bunch of friends who enjoyed me for who I was. We got really close, had parties, went trick-or-treating together on Halloween, celebrated each other's birthdays, stuff like that. And for the first time ever, *I* even had a party!

"It was a slumber party—four girls and one guy. The guy wasn't even in our group, but we invited him anyway. The way that happened was this: my friend Cordelia told me to come with her to her gym class, because she thought this one guy in the class named Max was gay.

"I went, and I agreed. I wanted to invite him, but he hadn't come out to anyone, so it was tricky. I mean, who knows? Maybe

When Joe gets tired of staying on the couch at his mother's place, he sometimes stays with his friend Angie (pictured).

he'd get really angry if he were invited to a slumber party with the gay and lesbian group if he was straight!"

Joe smiles, remembering.

"But we were both convinced he was gay. He was sort of soft, kind of limp-wristed. I don't believe people *look* gay; I think it's usually the mannerisms that can tell. Anyway, they were playing soccer in gym. He was the goalie. Not much of an athlete, he'd be yelling 'You go, girl!' to people on his team. Stuff like that.

"So Cordelia decided to approach him directly. We figured that was the only way to get him to tell, if we came right out and asked. So she went up to him and said, 'You know, Max, I like you a lot, and I've been hearing rumors that you were gay, and I was wondering if it was true. I mean, it doesn't matter to me; I just wanted to know.'

"He told her that he didn't know. She came running back and was yelling, 'He said he didn't know! That means he is!' It's funny—he ended up being my first boyfriend. I asked him later why he said he didn't know he was gay. He told me, 'Oh, I knew. I just wasn't about to tell you guys!'

"Anyway, the party was so much fun. We ate, laughed, played games like Truth or Dare. At one point I had to go into a closet with Max and exchange boxers! There was one girl who was going to be coming late on the bus, so I decided to go and meet her wearing a skirt. I had a jacket over it, but she didn't even notice—just said hi when she got off the bus. We walked over to my house, and when we were going up the steps, she finally noticed. I said, 'See?' And she was like, 'Whoa!' We laughed about that. I don't know, it was the most fun I think I'd had up to that point in my life."

MOVING HOME AND MOVING OUT

Just before his sixteenth birthday, Joe left the foster home to return to his mother's home.

"She wanted me back, and I knew she was really trying to stay straight," he explains. "I missed her, even though my life at school and socially was really great.

"She'd had a new baby, Amber, and she was really cute. And she was trying to hold down a part-time job. I'd baby-sit the girls while she was out and do my homework. It worked for a while, but I could tell that she was starting to slip up. She'd be out late then come home and go right upstairs to her room. I'd go up there; I knew what she was doing.

"A couple of months later, it had really gotten to me. I mean, she was spending the whole welfare check for drugs, she'd smoke it up in one weekend. Her hair was all wild, and she looked like shit. So one night I said, 'I'm leaving—come downstairs and watch the girls.' I packed my stuff and went to visit my stepmom."

Joe says that his leaving seemed to frighten his mother.

"When I got home she was really apologetic, really guilty," he says. "While I was gone, she bought me a brand-new bike. Mine had just been stolen, so I needed one. I told her thanks, but the bike wasn't going to change things too much. I said that if she did that again, started up on drugs and drinking like that, I would leave for good."

Joe shakes his head sadly.

"And she did, the very next weekend. I went upstairs and knocked on her door, and she opens it. Marijuana and all these other smells come wafting out. I'm like, 'Come downstairs now. I'm leaving!' I went to Duluth to visit my friend Cinta. She's seventeen, lives up there. I knew I'd be welcome, so I stayed a week or so.

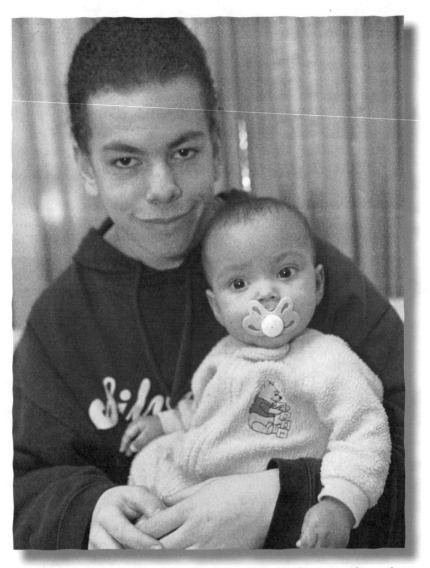

Between being sick and baby-sitting his sisters, Joe missed so many classes that he was kicked out of school.

"We didn't tell her parents why I was there. She was in school, but I'd wait for her until she got home; then we'd hang out. I'd take her car and go places while she was in class. I don't have my license or anything, but her parents never found out.

"And when I came home from Duluth, I didn't want to go back to my mom's. I mean, I missed her and the girls, but I was still so mad at her for what she was doing to our family. So I stayed with friends, a night here and there, anywhere I could stay."

KICKED OUT OF SCHOOL

Joe says that his mother's backsliding into drug addiction has cost him more than a family situation.

"I feel bad about not being able to live at home," he says, "but I feel just as bad about being kicked out of high school. I just missed so much school—between baby-sitting for the girls when my mom was out during the day and being sick during the month of October—they said I'd used up all the absences I was allowed. I had just enough absences so I'd fail every class, so I left."

Joe grins sheepishly.

"It wasn't like I was getting straight A's or anything. Far from it. I mean, I think of myself as pretty smart. I get good scores on those intelligence tests they give you. But I guess with my home life, and all the distractions, the moving around—I guess I have lacked concentration. I've gotten D's and F's when I should have been getting A's.

"My favorite classes were pop choir and this one class called Art Smart. Art Smart was really fun. It wasn't drawing, and that's

In high school, one of Joe's favorite classes was pop choir. He sang bass and baritone, and he enjoyed the concerts and recitals. Although he's no longer in school, Joe continues to dabble in music.

good, because I don't draw well. You just learn about art and what makes certain paintings good.

"And I sing bass in the choir, or baritone if they need extras. We did a lot of cool stuff in there—lots of concerts and recitals. One bad thing that happened was that on one of the days I missed school because of my mom, our choir got to perform for the governor. I wasn't there, and I felt bad about it.

"If I go back to school next trimester, I'm not sure if I could get back in choir, and that worries me. The teacher doesn't like me at all, and I swear to God I don't know why. It's not just me—everyone in there knows he doesn't like me. I don't think it's because of me being gay. That would be too weird. I guess it will all depend on whether he needs more men's voices in the choir. But he'd choose a monotone over me, I know it."

Joe smiles and shrugs his shoulders.

"I guess I'll worry about that when the time comes, huh?"

SOCIAL LIFE

Joe says he really misses the kids in his gay and lesbian group at school but that he occasionally sees a few of the kids outside of school.

"I miss seeing Cordelia," he says. "We were best friends for a while, but that sort of fell apart before I left school. When more and more girls started joining that group at school, she sort of dropped me for them. We hardly call each other anymore, and that hurts. But I've made some new friends. I really like going to Duluth to see Cinta, and I hang out with Angie and Becca."

As far as boyfriends, Joe says that he had a relationship with Max, but that is over.

"I broke up with Max because I loved him," he admits. "That sounds sort of strange, but it's true. I felt like I was too young to be in love, and I hadn't been with enough people to really know. Max doesn't talk to me much either. I think he's mad because I told people we'd broken up. I don't know. He never told people that we were going together in the first place, so maybe he was really uncomfortable about it.

"At first when we broke up, I was really upset about not being with him anymore. I used to think about him all the time. I'd cruise by his mom's house and then his dad's—his parents were divorced. I had a route all worked out. But now I'm over him. He

Since being kicked out of school, Joe says he misses his friends from the gay and lesbian group. He has made some new friends, though, including Angie (center) and Cinta (right).

was the only guy I've ever gone out with that I cared about that much. He was special. I mean, I lost my virginity to him, so that's a big deal. He was the first."

He has had five relationships since Max, he says, but none of them has proved as meaningful as Max.

"I had a self-esteem problem for a while," Joe says, "and I'd have a tendency to sabotage relationships if they seemed like they were too good. I went out with this one guy, Tim, and he was great. I liked him, he liked me, and all his friends liked me. It was just too perfect, and I guess I just didn't believe that I deserved something that good. So I broke up with him.

"Since that, I've gone out with people that I'd normally never go out with. I was like, desperate. I was so unsure of myself that I thought I needed these guys. I wouldn't even classify them as re-lationships, just guys. They were friends, and then I went out with them. That's just how it's been going for me."

"It's Hard to Be a Sixteen-Year-Old Gay Kid"

Joe says without pause that his life is not an easy one.

"I'm not feeling sorry for myself," he says. "But it's really hard to be a sixteen-year-old gay kid. There's all that sex involved, that kind of stuff. Everyone my age, all they want is sex it seems like. The gay guys more than the straight, I think. I don't know why that is. Most gay kids, all they think about is sex.

"I like having friends; I like the closeness of that. I'd like to know someone a long time before having sex with him. I just don't know how to handle it sometimes, I really don't. I'm sure straight kids might go through some of the same stuff, but I don't think it's as hard for them.

"I don't get harassed much, unless I'm doing something like wearing really tight clothes. Sometimes it's fun to dress up. But I've never been in a fight or anything. I mean, there was that thing with the Tabasco sauce in the group home, but that was a group home, and those kids are supposed to be asses, you know?

"I mean, sometimes I've gotten looks when my hair has been growing out for a long time. Sometimes I get asked if I'm a boy or a girl. I remember this one time a guy was looking me over, trying to get me to talk to see whether I had a deep voice. He asked me what time it was. I knew just what he was doing. He wasn't rude enough to ask if I was a girl; he just wanted to know. I just said, 'Hmmmm.'"

The other part that Joe says has been difficult at times is dealing with his family.

"Like I said, my mom already knows. She says she's always known. And Stefan . . . well, I told you what he's like. My real dad knows, but I didn't tell him; my social worker did. Can you believe that? With his new religion and everything, I know he hates that I'm gay. He doesn't accept it, but he told me he loves me anyway. Maybe that's something, but it doesn't feel like much.

"My one aunt thinks maybe I am, but I haven't said anything to her, and I know my mom hasn't. She just got religion, too, so she wouldn't acknowledge my sexuality. She just wouldn't want to deal with it. If I'm not always talking about a girl, she'll do the same thing my stepdad does, kind of. She'll ask me these leading questions about who I'm seeing, and stuff like that. She knows about my friends Cinta and Angie, and she's trying to make that a romantic thing.

"The worst one to tell would be my grandpa. I hope he never finds out. He's real old-fashioned, really just a guy-guy, you know? He'd never talk to me again, and he'd probably take me out of his will. It just wouldn't be worth it to bring it up."

"FIND OUT ALL YOU CAN"

"I feel real bad about the fact that I'm probably never going to live with my mother and sisters again," says Joe sadly. "I don't even know how long they'll let her keep the girls. I'm convinced that treatment just won't work for her. I mean, she's been through it so

Joe is a meticulous scheduler. He lives by his planner, which he carries around like a wallet or purse.

many times, and nothing's really happened. She's just going to keep backsliding, and it would make no difference if I were there or not. She'll just keep it up, keep losing us."

He says that he has no plans for the future, other than trying to enroll back at his high school next term.

"I can't even imagine what it would be like to know what you were going to do five or ten years from now," he says. "I've never been able to do that. I'm not sure where I fit in, what kind of things I'd even be good at.

"I *do* know that I've learned some things in the last sixteen years, though. I mean, I've learned that most counselors at these youth shelters and social agencies are worthless. I've been to plenty of them. And after I talk to them a while, I'm saying to myself, 'Oh, wow, I could do this same thing with my best friend.' These guys have no answers. Plus, I'd rather talk to someone that I know I could trust."

Joe leans forward in his chair.

"I think kids are better off getting their strength from inside themselves. If I could think of something to tell kids that are struggling with the realization that they're gay, I'd say they should find out all they can about it. Go to the library, look in the Yellow Pages. I mean, there are places you can go to talk to people who understand. Find out all you can before you open your mouth to anyone. That's what I'd say."

Justin

"WHEN YOU'RE YOUNG, YOU THINK YOU'RE SO DIFFERENT, SO ISOLATED FROM EVERYONE ELSE. AND THEN . . . YOU FIND OUT THERE ARE OTHER PEOPLE OUT THERE WITH THE SAME FEELINGS."

At first it is difficult getting anything more than one-word answers from Justin. A tall, good-looking boy who looks younger than his seventeen years, he is wearing jeans and a black-and-white Adidas soccer jacket. His sandy hair is hidden by a maroon baseball cap with the name Harvard on the front.

"It's hard for me to talk to people I don't know," he says in a deep voice, smiling and blushing furiously. "It doesn't matter what I'm talking about, I get real shy. Maybe it's because I grew up in a little town or something . . . I don't know."

Justin laughs nervously.

"Where I grew up is called Marine. Most people have never even heard of it, even though it's like half an hour from the city. Marine is just a little river town, with not much to do. It's pretty boring, in fact. There's nothing there for anybody to do. The kids go to another town to hang out, and when they get their licenses, they sometimes go to the city. In fact, that's where I'm going to be living as soon as I graduate from high school.

"I'm the youngest in our family. I have a brother and two sisters. The oldest sister is thirty-two, so you could say there was really a big span in there. My dad is retired now, but he used to work for a company that makes windows for houses. My mom is an elementary school librarian."

"Honest, I've Known Since I Was Eight!"

Justin is gay, and he insists he has known since he was eight years old.

"I know it sounds too young, but it's true," he says. "I knew back then I didn't like girls. I had lots of girls that liked me, but I really didn't like them.

"Most of my friends did, though. Third grade . . . I don't know, but at our school that was the time when boys asked girls to go out with you, you know. I liked boys more. I'd want to spend time with them better. But I never told anybody, though. Sometimes my friends would say, 'Hey Justin, why don't you get a girlfriend, too?' And I'd say, 'Because I don't want one.' And they'd drop it. That would be that."

Justin says that unlike many elementary school–age boys, he knew what the word *gay* meant.

"My older sister had a friend who was different from other boys I knew," he says. "This is when I was eight or nine. I didn't know the word yet, but I could recognize that this guy was really different. He never had girlfriends, but he seemed to have boyfriends. I mean, he had a lot of girls that he hung around with. He seemed more comfortable talking to girls, like my sister and her friends.

"He didn't seem effeminate or anything, just a regular guy. But he'd be sitting next to a boy he'd come over with, and he'd be touching him on the leg, always touching him. I mean, when you're a little boy, you know that's weird, touching other boys on the leg.

"So I asked my sister about that guy—how come he didn't have any girlfriends, why he was touching that other boy like that. She told me, 'Because he's gay.' I asked her what that meant, and she told me it's when you like people of the same sex in a romantic way."

A Hard Time

Even though Justin had no romantic interests in other boys when he was in elementary school, he says that things changed a lot when he went to junior high.

"The kids from Marine went to a different school for junior high; we went into that bigger town nearby," he explains. "That was a lot more exciting, but it was a really hard time for me. For

Justin lives at home with his parents. With the help of his sister, Justin has told his mom that he is gay, but he has never actually told his dad.

one thing, there was a lot more pressure to take girls out. Everyone wanted to know who was going with who, who liked who.

"Like I said, I never had a girlfriend. If a girl liked me, I just avoided her. Like if I found out a girl thought I was cute or something, I'd just stop talking to her. It wasn't to be mean or anything—just because I thought it was a bad idea to pretend, you know? First thing you know, a girl tells one of her friends, and then she tells me that so and so likes me, and what do I think of her, stuff like that. I didn't want to be involved in that stuff at all.

"And my guy friends would always be trying to fix me up with a girl. That was really uncomfortable. They'd be talking about girls and which ones they thought were really hot. I'd sit there, kind of pretending to be interested, but I wasn't at all. They tried fixing me up with this girl Annie. I liked her, but not in that way."

Justin smiles, remembering.

"It was kind of funny. Years later, when I started coming out to people, she was one of the people I trusted. When I told her about me, she told me she knew. One of her friends had told her a long time ago!"

ATTRACTED TO BOYS

Justin says it was in junior high that he first started being sexually interested in boys at school.

"I didn't know most of the kids at school," he says. "Just the ones who came from Marine like me. So I saw these new boys and started kind of getting feelings about them when I'd see them in the locker room changing for gym class. Some of them looked cute to me, and I was sneaking looks at them. I liked how they looked, and I never had those feelings about girls. I don't know. It's not real easy to explain; it's just how I felt."

Justin says that he never acted on any of those feelings—quite the opposite. Such feelings, he insists, made him feel depressed.

"I felt so weird all the time," he says. "I felt like I must be the only kid in the world right then who felt like that. I realized that it was kids like me that other kids made fag jokes about. I knew that if anyone found out that I felt like this, I'd have absolutely no friends left. I didn't want to be one of those kids—the ones who always sit by themselves at lunch, way off in a corner of the lunchroom. I didn't know what I'd do.

"Another thing that made it scary is that there was this one kid I knew named Jimmy. He was gay, although he hadn't come out or anything. But he was real effeminate, talked real different from the other kids. He uses his hands a lot. I don't know; it's hard to describe, but if you saw him talking, you'd just know he was gay. It wasn't the words he used or anything. It wasn't like he was real smart. Just the way he said words, just the way his voice went up and down."

Justin remembers that Jimmy was ridiculed by many boys at school.

"He was a really nice guy," says Justin, "but it was kind of dangerous being around him. All the guys who were my friends used to ask me why I hung around with him. He got teased all the time and called names. Kids tried to beat him up, too—even some of my friends! I never joined in, but I didn't really stick up for him, either. I do know that my face always got red when someone said the word *faggot*.

"So anyway, when I saw how Jimmy was treated by other people at school, especially my friends, I knew there was no way I wanted anybody to know I was gay. So I just got more and more depressed, not knowing who to trust, worrying about what I'd do, what would happen, feeling so different."

Eighth grade was even worse than seventh, Justin says. The constant pressure he felt from his peers to get a girlfriend, or to explain why he wasn't interested in girls, got more intense.

SKIPPING SCHOOL

"I hated the pretending," he says. "So how I handled it was that me and some friends of mine just started not going to school. We'd get up every morning and take the bus like we were going to school, but we'd just walk out before first period. And I'm not talking about a few days here, it was nine weeks!"

When asked how he and his friends could be absent for that much time without getting in trouble, he shrugs.

"We'd call in for each other every day, pretending to be each other's father or mother. I had a friend who was a student assistant in the office, and she'd just mark me down as if my mom had called in or that I had mono or something that would take me a long time to recover from. I don't exactly remember feeling bad or guilty. Maybe I was going through a rebel phase or something.

"We didn't have any trouble passing the time, that's for sure. We mostly hung out at Jody's house, because she lived a half block from school. And that worked out, because by the time we walked over there from school, her mom was gone. She worked all day, see, so it was perfect.

"It was me, Jody, a girl named Carey, and a boy named Jeremy. He was a year younger. We'd just talk, watch television, stuff like that. Jeremy was the youngest, so he was our runner. He'd run from Jody's house to the store and get us cigarettes, doughnuts, stuff like that. He knew a guy at the store—that's how he could get the cigarettes. And at lunchtime, we'd either order pizza and have it delivered, or we'd send Jeremy to the other end of town to get subs and pop."

Justin grins, "We kind of had it made, for a while!"

He says that although most of what they did was just talk and fool around, he never brought up the issue that troubled him most.

"I never confided in them," he says. "I just wasn't ready, even though I really liked them. I mean, they were good friends, and they'd probably have stuck by me, but I just couldn't say anything. Jody would ask me. She'd ask me all the time, 'Are you gay, Justin?' But I'd say no. I just couldn't risk having my secret out, so that someone at school could find out."

BUSTED

For nine weeks, says Justin, no one from school called their homes to check on them.

"We were really pulling it off," Justin declares with a hint of pride. "But we sort of screwed up one day by walking up to the high school. See, my friend Jody wanted to see someone that she knew up there. Anyway, the cops stopped us and asked us where we were going, what we thought we were doing. Obviously, we looked too young to be in high school. That's why they stopped us.

"My friend got kind of smart with the cops. I think she told them that she'd dropped out of school because she was sixteen, or something. I don't even know. Anyway, the one cop called her mother to see what was going on. Her mom was completely surprised and said she was supposed to be in school.

"The cops took us to the junior high, and we waited to go into the office one at a time. I was first and was really getting yelled at. Jody and Carey were listening outside, and they got scared because of all the yelling. So they took off. They went to Jody's house to pack her stuff, and they came down the stairs, and who do they bump into? Her mom. She was so mad that she took them right back to school so they could get yelled at, too. Jody got kicked out, and the rest of us were told that we'd be sent away if we ever tried anything like that again."

TELLING THE SECRET

Justin says that when he started high school, he finally decided to tell a couple of close friends about his sexuality. He didn't want it to get around, however, and he swore his friends to secrecy.

"They were fine about it," he says. "And it's funny how all of a sudden I needed to tell them. I was just so tired of lying, of pretending. I told Jimmy; he'd come out earlier. And I told a friend of his. I was surprised that they both knew."

Justin laughs and looks baffled.

"I guess my big dark secret wasn't so secret after all, huh? Anyway, Jimmy's friend asked me if I wanted to come with her to this place in the city called 202. It's like a social place just for gay, lesbian, and bisexual teens. No adults, except the ones that run the place. I didn't know at first. I mean, I'd only talked about this with two people. But it couldn't hurt, I figured, so we decided to go the next weekend.

"The place was really crowded, and I met this one guy almost right away. He kept trying to talk to me, but I was so shy, I didn't talk to him. Anyway, at the end of the evening, the guy asked me for my phone number, and I gave it to him."

Justin shakes his head in disgust.

"Big mistake, though. I mean, he turned out to be really annoying. He called all the time, nonstop, morning, afternoon, all night. It got to the point where my mom was asking me who that guy was that kept calling all the time. I learned after that. I bought a pager. Whenever I'd meet someone that I thought I maybe wanted to get to know, I just gave them my pager number!"

FIRST DATE

Justin says that his first relationship was not with someone from 202, but rather someone he met in a gay bar in the city.

"I went there with a couple of friends that I'd told," he says. "This was several months later, when I'd told some other people, mostly girls I was really close to. Anyway, this was a bar that used to be real casual about checking IDs. They practically never did.

"So anyway, I was sitting there with my friends, and I notice this one guy I thought was really cute. He was black, had a shaved head, and two gold loop earrings. He dressed good, too—baggy pants, and a shirt tucked in. I was really nervous, though. I mean, I'd never approached anyone before.

"I asked my friend Sarah if she'd go up and talk to him, maybe bring him back to our table so we could talk. So she did. He came right over, and we talked for a few minutes. His name was Tyrone, and it turned out that he was just leaving. He said he was studying to be a flight attendant, and he had to do some studying. But he told me he'd call me later, so I guess that was kind of nice."

Justin says that Tyrone invited him to come over to his apartment the next day, but as usual, his shyness really got in the way.

"Sarah went with me because I was so scared, too nervous to go over there by myself," he says. "We got there, and it was this really nice apartment building. I was so nervous that I tripped and fell down the stairs! This was the first time for me, so you can kind of understand. Sarah understood, but she was laughing so hard at me.

"Anyway, we got into his apartment, and he seemed really glad to see me. He offered us beer, but me and Sarah don't drink, so we just kind of sat there. I didn't talk all night. I don't think I said a word. But Sarah talked the entire time, talked enough for all three of us."

Justin says that the following days were less stressful.

"He called the next day, and we just talked a lot. I really liked him, so we saw each other again, and this time we talked a lot. He was a nice guy, bought me lots of stuff I didn't even ask for. No

Justin and a friend laugh while playing with his teddy bear collection. With the support of his friends, Justin was able to be more open about his homosexuality.

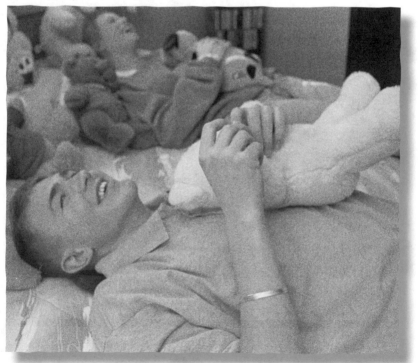

one had ever done that for me before. I mean, he sent me money in the mail, gave me teddy bears, took me to this great amusement park. He even bought me a gold chain with a matching gold bracelet.

"Anyway, he moved back to New York when he finished flight attendant school, so we don't really see each other anymore. He calls me several times a week, but that's it. I have a new boyfriend named Larry, so I have no interest in getting back with Tyrone. Plus, he was older than me. I was sixteen, and he was twenty-nine. That's a big gap, you know?"

FINDING LARRY

He has been together with Larry a long time now, and Justin says he really loves him a lot.

"I met him at 202," he explains. "Or I should say, I saw him there. He was working as a DJ one night, playing music for the dancing. I thought he was really cute. He's black. I guess I'm really attracted to black guys. All the guys I've ever been interested in or have thought about have been black.

"Anyway, I asked my friend who that guy was, and she knew his name. So one day not long after that, I saw him at the mall, and we got talking. I was there with my friend Sarah, and he was with this guy named Nathan. Larry and I dropped Nathan and Sarah off together, which made Sarah kind of mad. I mean, she knew Larry and I liked each other, but she didn't want to be stuck with Nathan. She didn't like him, and she liked him a lot less when she found out he was married!

"I guess we both knew right away that we liked each other. He's a little older than me. He works as a singer around town, even works for Prince sometimes. He just made his own demo tape, and he gave me a copy. He's a great dancer, too. He used to get into lots of clubs even though he was too young, because his dancing was really good for their business. They liked him."

Now, he says, they're very serious about each another. They spend most of their free time together, and as a result, Justin felt as if he were ready to come out to his friends at school whom he'd never told.

"It seemed important now, because of Larry," he says simply. "Like I said before, I was tired of pretending and lying, especially around my friends who are guys. These were the guys who were always calling, the ones I ski with, or rent movies with, just drive around with and hang out. But it was getting harder and harder to come up with excuses, because I wanted to spend time with Larry.

"Some of them were okay about it; they didn't seem all that surprised. But I did lose some friends. I mean, they didn't run away from me or anything. But they just sort of slowly pulled away from me, stopped talking with me or sitting with me. It wasn't most of my friends, but it was enough to hurt a lot."

As hard as that had been, however, Justin knew that he needed to be open with his family. And that was going to be very hard.

"THEY JUST ASSUMED HE WAS ONE OF MY FRIENDS"

"I kept thinking about how to tell my parents," says Justin, "but I couldn't think of a way. I was afraid of what they'd say, afraid they'd be angry or sad. So in a way it was kind of a relief that I never really had to tell either one of them. My sister was the one, and that was fine with me.

"She was visiting up here from Florida. She's the one who's thirty-two, the one who had a really close gay friend up here before she moved. Anyway, this was about six months ago. Larry had been sending little messages on my pager, like 'I love you,' and stuff like that. And she was looking at the messages, trying to figure out what they said. She was really confused, too. She kept saying, 'Who's this from?' I told her, 'Larry.' She said, 'Oh.' She didn't get it at all, even though I was hoping she'd just figure it out without my saying anything.

"Anyway, later me and Larry were talking on the phone. I handed her the phone, and let her talk to him. I was thinking maybe he would say something, and she'd figure it out."

Justin snaps his fingers.

"I should have told you that my sister had met Larry already, from when she had visited last Christmas. Really, everyone in my family had met Larry. He came over a lot, but of course, they just assumed he was one of my friends. But they all liked him a lot. He was friendly and easy to talk to. And the fact that he was black, well, it was a really big deal that my family got past that, especially my dad.

"See, my mom is fine, but my dad is really a racist. I don't think he means to be, but really, until I started bringing Larry over, I

68

When Justin finally told his friends he was gay, he said that some of them "just sort of slowly pulled away from me. . . . It wasn't most of my friends, but it was enough to hurt a lot."

don't think he'd ever talked to a black person in his life. All his ideas about black guys came from TV. So when I brought Larry over the first time, my dad was nice—I mean, he'd never be mean—but you could tell he didn't really like black people.

"But my dad figured out that Larry wasn't a gangbanger or a drug dealer or anything else he saw on TV, just a regular person. So I guess you could say that my dad had a nice surprise. He got over his racism pretty quick. I mean, he never would say anything like 'Larry is not welcome in our house,' because he's not like that. But he started warming up to Larry, talking more when Larry came around. My mom never had a problem, because she's from the city. Not like my dad, who's been in the country all his life."

A ROUNDABOUT WAY OF COMING OUT

Justin has rambled off the subject, and he pauses a moment in confusion, wondering where all this was leading.

"Oh, yeah," he smiles, blushing. "So my sister knew Larry already and liked him. So when they were talking, I got on the extension, and we were all three of us talking. And finally she figured it out. And she was shocked, really shocked. She started laughing real hard—not because it was funny, but because she wasn't sure what to do, I think.

"So my sister starts asking me questions, like how long we've been seeing each other and how long I've known I was gay. She got over her shock real fast and wanted me to know she supported me. Like I said, she has had good friends that were gay, so she didn't think it was weird or anything.

"I asked her if she wanted to tell my mom. I told her that I hadn't told anyone in the family yet, because it was hard for me. So anyway, the next morning, I got up and went into the kitchen. And there were my sister and my mom, talking. I knew they were talking about me, and I didn't want to be there. My sister told me later that my mom was crying, and I sure am glad I didn't see that.

"So anyway, my mom came into my room a while later and told me that she loved me and that she would always be supportive of me. Like I said, she really liked Larry, so that part was a little easier than if I had a stranger as a boyfriend. But she didn't resent Larry or say anything bad about him."

"MY FATHER WOULD NEVER REACT THAT WAY"

Justin still has not told his father, although he suspects his father knows.

"I know some kids have real trouble when they finally tell their parents. I've heard stories of kids getting kicked out of the house or of their parents calling them bad names, especially their fathers. My father would never react that way, I know. Even if it really bothered him, he wouldn't get mad. He's real quiet and just as shy as me.

"One of the things I worried about was that it would shock him; I didn't want him to have another heart attack or anything. He had two already, the last one just a month ago. I don't know . . . I don't think I've ever been real close to him. He was closer to my older brother and my sisters. I guess I was too little to do the things they did, or something. Because I'm the youngest, I spent more time with my mom. We like to shop," he says with a laugh.

"But don't get me wrong. I love my dad. He just has different interests than I do. He likes to hunt and fish. I mean, I'll fish but

I've never been hunting. And he goes to bed like at eight o'clock every night. He's real religious, too. But we go out sometimes together on the boat, stuff like that. But I don't feel like I can just start talking to him about something like being gay.

"But I think he knows. Maybe my mom told him, or maybe he just has figured it out. The other night I was leaving the house, and my dad says, 'Aren't you and Larry still seeing each other?' My mom says, 'Of course they are' and she sort of takes over the conversation. So I just left. Maybe sometimes we'll both feel comfortable about things, but I'm not sure."

"HE'D USE THE PHRASE 'STUPID FAGS' A LOT"

Justin hasn't told his other sister or his brother, either, and has no plans to do so in the near future. Although he and his brother, Jason, are close, he's not sure how Jason would react.

"He was the biggest jock in high school," says Justin. "Totally different from me. I've never gone out for any sports in school. But Jason was into lots of stuff—football, weight lifting, you name

Shopping is one of Justin's favorite pastimes.

it. I mean, he was second place in the nation for lifting when he was a senior in high school.

"We didn't get along very well a few years ago, when I was in eighth grade and he was a senior. He was always real opinionated about people. He got real mad at me when he found out I was smoking. He used to say that all smokers should just die, that they were no good. So he'd yell at me and pin me down and threaten to beat me up if I didn't stop. And he was one of the guys who were real big on using *fag* to describe people. He'd use the phrase 'stupid fags' a lot, in fact. It was a big joke with him. In his view, all fags should just be killed."

Justin and Jason have gotten along better in recent months, however. Perhaps, says Justin, it's because they're both older and a little more mature.

"We do stuff together sometimes now," he says. "Like we go over to the fitness center and work out with weights, stuff like that. He seems nicer about things. It's funny, because he was as racist as my dad, but Jason really likes Larry. He'd never talked to a black person before, either. But now he gets along great with Larry.

"I switched high schools recently, and Jason asked me all kinds of questions about whether people were giving me problems. I told him no, that everything was okay. I mean, the truth was that I left my high school because I didn't feel comfortable there after coming out. But I didn't tell Jason that. But he was saying things like, 'You let me know if you're having trouble with any guys, because I'll take care of them.' He could, too, because he's really built like a weight lifter still, even though he's out of high school."

When asked whether Jason would still offer protection if Justin were to come out to him, Justin is unsure.

"I think he'd take care of it," he says. "He'd go after anyone who was hassling me because he's my brother and that's a family thing. But I don't know, it does make me pretty nervous, thinking about telling him that I'm gay. I can't guarantee that he's changed *that* much."

STEREOTYPES

Justin is sure that negative stereotypes are responsible for much of the prejudice people have toward gay people. However, he is optimistic that such stereotypes can be overcome.

"I really believe that the thinking that made my brother and my dad racists is the same for people who are prejudiced towards gays," he says. "People just assume that if you're gay, you think of all guys as potential boyfriends, and that's stupid. Like the guys at my old high school that started ignoring me after I told them. I went back there one time because there are people there who are still my friends. I just wanted to kind of talk to them, see how things were going.

"But they're kind of distant, even the ones who are still friendly. It makes them uncomfortable, so they just stay away from that subject. They just don't talk about it. It's like I never mentioned it to them. In fact, one of my old friends said, "Boy, I hope you didn't like *me!*' That's the kind of level they're on, I guess."

CHANGING MINDS

A lot of the blame, he says, comes from the media misrepresenting gay people.

"I notice it more and more," he complains. "Especially on talk shows like *Jerry Springer* and shows like that. Every guy who's gay dresses in drag; he's never a normal-looking person. They just like to get in the audience's face, just so the audience will hoot at them. The more flamboyant the better, and I don't think that's fair.

"I know there are some gay people that are like that—my friend Jimmy, for one. I mean, he crosses his legs and sits there talking with his hands, talking just like those guys on TV. And he can do the limp wrist thing and the walk. But that's not me, and it's sure not a lot of other gay people.

"But as mad as I get, I know that those stereotypes can be erased if people get to know some gay people. Like my friend Carey. We went to her sister's house, and her sister's boyfriend Matt had never met a gay person. He didn't know I was gay, either. Well, there's a bunch of guys that hang out over there all the time, and they would sometimes say stuff about gay people that we'd be seeing on TV, and stuff like that. One time after I'd left, Carey's sister told them that I was gay. I think she thought that it might make things more comfortable for me if they knew.

"Anyway, those guys were really surprised; they said they'd never have thought I was gay. Carey's sister told me that they told her that I totally changed their ideas about gay people. I thought that was pretty cool. They were so closed-minded before, but after

Justin is sure that he knew he was gay when he was eight. "A lot of girls liked me, but I didn't like them."

getting to know me, they were fine with it. So now, I hear that if Matt is around someone who says something negative about gay people or makes a crack about faggots or something, he sticks up for the gay person! It's like he's an expert or something now, and Carey says he acts real proud of himself."

"I THINK WE REALLY HAVE A FUTURE TOGETHER"

Justin takes out his wallet, which is brimming with pictures of friends and family.

"This is my sister; here's my mom," he says excitedly. "And that's my sister's son. He's really cute, huh?"

He tosses a few pictures out of the wallet, dismissing them as unimportant.

"These are kids I used to know, but we don't see each other anymore. This one is my friend Sarah. And this," he says, "is Larry."

Larry is a handsome man with a confident, self-possessed look on his face.

"I really think we have a future together," says Justin. "We're together nonstop—all the time. We shop a lot, because we both love doing that. We go to movies, to his studio where he works. I go with him when he DJs some nights and sit with him. We go out and eat a lot.

"Someone asked me how big a worry AIDS or HIV was to me. I guess I'm not worried at all. I mean, I know he's only with me.

Justin loves to show off his pictures. His duffel bag is filled with photos of his friends.

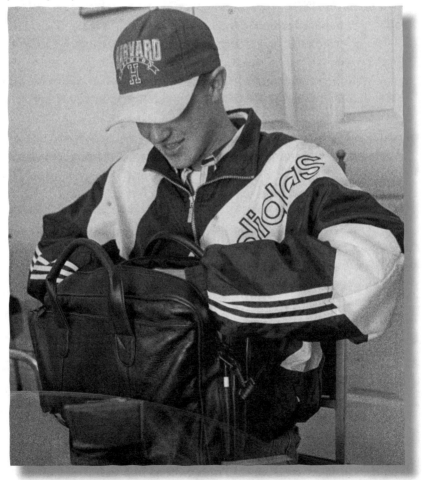

He's with me all the time, so I know he has no time to see anyone else! Plus, he's really quiet, not someone who is always out there looking for a new boyfriend. I mean, there are a lot of guys like that, but he's not. We plan on living together, like I said before."

FIGHTING SOMETIMES

Do they ever fight? Justin smiles and blushes.

"Oh yeah, we do sometimes. Not real often, but sometimes. We broke up for about a month before Christmas. It was all a misunderstanding, though. No real reason. Larry didn't think I wanted to be with him, just because I didn't say that I did. He wants me to say things, and sometimes it's hard to be real open.

"We ended up getting back together pretty quick. He called on Christmas Eve to wish me and my family Merry Christmas, and we talked then. We made plans to go to see *Waiting to Exhale* after Christmas, and then things were fine.

"It took me a long time to get used to being affectionate in public. I mean, we don't kiss or anything, but sometimes when we're walking around at the mall, or something, we hold hands, just kind of discreetly. My friend Sarah used to get kind of uncomfortable being with us, I think. I mean, Larry is a toucher. But Sarah has gotten used to it, and I'm more comfortable, too. I think the fact that I was sometimes less willing to be affectionate at first hurt his feelings.

"I mean, not that long ago we got into a big fight right outside his house. We were in his car, and I was mad at him for something—again, something really insignificant. Larry never knows what to do when I'm mad, so he yells. He kept yelling and yelling, really loud, and I started crying. So neither of us knew what to do. He yelled more, because he was real nervous. And I cried harder, because I was nervous, too.

"Anyway, he stormed out of the car and whipped a plastic bottle that he was carrying against the side of his house. All the neighbors were looking at us, too. We made up like five hours later, and everything was fine. I guess it's no different than any couple. You just fight and make up."

LOOKING AHEAD

Justin has some definite ideas about his future, although he concedes that it's possible that things could work out far differently than he assumes now.

Justin wants to become a buyer for a department store. That way he will be able to turn his love of shopping into a career.

"I'm going to graduate earlier than most kids my age," he says proudly. "Like I said before, when all the kids at my high school were acting weird about my being gay, I decided to transfer. It wasn't automatic, getting into this new school, either. I mean, usually you have to have a real reason for going there, like you're always in trouble, or on drugs or something. They let you work as fast or as slow as you want, and I guess that style is good for some kids.

"They asked me when I applied why I wanted to go there, and I said it was personal. I don't need anyone knowing my business.

My mom asked me if it was because of my being gay, and I said yeah. So she put 'personal' on the form, too, and signed it."

After high school, Justin says he has plans to become a buyer for men's clothing at an upscale department store.

"I know you need two years of college for that," he says, "and then two years of apprenticeship. But it's right up my line. I mean, ever since I was real young, I've loved to go shopping with my mom. And now, I'm working and I'm able to buy great clothes at a discount. It's fun, and as a buyer, I'd earn pretty good money."

"I KNOW I'M NOT ONE TO TALK"

Justin says that he thinks a lot about the past three years and how that time was so difficult for him. It has made him reevaluate how he handled things, and he admits he wishes he had been brave enough to tell people sooner about his sexuality.

"I think about how so many kids in my high school and junior high were so mean to kids like Jimmy, and then to me. I mean, I didn't get the all-out abuse he did, but I felt it from some people.

Although Justin swore no one else in his high school was gay, he has recently seen some old classmates in local gay bars. "I guess you can't assume anything in high school, right?"

When you're young, you think you're so different, so isolated from everyone else. And then in a couple of years, things change. You find out there are other people out there with the same feelings."

Justin laughs, remembering something he was trying to recall earlier.

"It was pretty funny when I started going to some of the clubs and gay bars in the city," he says. "I had been so sure in my old high school that I was the only guy that was gay, especially after Jimmy had changed schools. But since then I've seen a couple of guys and one girl from my school at that same gay bar! The one guy was wearing lipstick and blue eye shadow, and his fingernails were all polished."

He smiles. "I guess you can't assume anything in high school, right? If I had it to do over again, I'd have done things differently. I mean, if I knew a kid who was in junior high and was going through all that stuff now—sneaking looks at other kids, stuff like that—I'd tell that kid to stop worrying. Just be yourself. If people don't like you, they'll stay away. Of course, at first they might hassle you, but eventually they'll stay away.

"Give yourself some time, too. If you know absolutely in your heart that you're gay, sit down and talk to your parents if you can. I know I'm not one to talk, being as secretive and everything that I was. But I'll tell you, I'd have saved myself a lot of sad, sad times, just lying in bed at night and worrying. I guess I've learned the hard way. But I've learned, and that's something."

Nikki

"I WANT TO BE AS HONEST WITH
PEOPLE AS I CAN. . . . THE MORE
I CAN SHOW PEOPLE THAT I'M
NOT SO DIFFERENT FROM THEM,
THAT I'M NOT ABNORMAL, THEY
CAN LEARN TO BE MORE
ACCEPTING."

Nikki is comfortable talking about being a lesbian, being a college student, human rights, or anything else. She's a bubbly twenty-year-old who has led, by her own admission, a "perfectly charmed life."

"I know I'm really talkative," she says with a grin. "If I go on and on, just stop me. But I'm really excited to be telling my story, because there's this notion out there that to be lesbian or gay must mean a person has experienced abuse as a child, suicidal feelings, or at the very least, bouts of clinical depression.

"Not me. In a way, sometimes, I feel guilty that I haven't experienced some of the angst [anxiety] that I've read about in the gay community. But to be honest, I'm very happy. I wouldn't want to change a thing about myself. That might change someday, but for now, it's true."

"ALL MY MEMORIES ARE VERY GOOD"

Nikki is Korean, adopted when she was six months old by a middle-class couple from the suburbs. Although many young people who are adopted sometimes have feelings of anger or confusion over being given up by birth parents, Nikki insists she has never had a problem, either with her being adopted, or with being Korean in a very white environment.

"I don't remember ever being teased when I was little," she says. "I mean, there were the usual things growing up Korean in a white area—kids making slanty-eyes at me, stuff like that. But I don't think there was anything more than that. My parents had a biological son after I arrived, so I always had someone to play with. Our neighborhood was nice, full of kids, so there was always something fun going on. Really, all my memories are very good.

"I don't know if I was popular in school when I was growing up. I don't know if I even thought in those terms. But I always had friends around me. I had a small core of friends that were my close friends, the ones you can tell anything to. And there was the outer group of friends that we'd do things with. I never remember feeling left out."

Nikki says that her family has always been as important to her as her friends.

"My mom I consider my absolute best friend, and she always has been. Both my mom and dad have played really major roles in my life. She's worked on and off part-time when my brother and I were younger. She stayed home as much as she could with us. My dad teaches at a nearby technical school.

"Our family has always been close, and that has been a real plus in my life. In fact, my mom thinks that my self-confidence comes from the fact that I was always treated as if what I had to say was important. I never remember feeling that my parents were bored when I told them about things at school or games I was playing or anything like that.

"My brother is similar to me in temperament. He is perhaps a little quieter, but he's not afraid to speak his mind. I like that a lot. We don't get to see each other as much now, because he's going to college in Wisconsin.

"School has always been fun for me. I haven't always breezed through every class or anything, but I've enjoyed it. The teachers have been good. I still love school—so much that I'm reluctant to think about graduation in another year! I think I'm one of those people who could just stay in school forever, taking different classes, meeting new people. It's a good environment for me, I think."

THE ONLY GIRL CADDY

Nikki has junior status at the university, although she is only in her second year. She was lucky enough to receive a four-year scholarship called the Evans Scholarship—for being a golf caddy.

"I've been caddying since I was fifteen," she says smiling. "I took it up when I realized that there were just a few jobs fifteen-year-olds could have. Baby-sitting was boring, and I didn't want to mow lawns, so I applied at a nearby country club to be a caddy.

"I was the only girl there," she says, "although by the time I left for college, there were a couple of other girls. I loved it. You walked around on this beautiful course, the sun was shining, everything was so pretty. And then you get paid in cash!

"And no," she says with a laugh, "I'm not a golfer. I own a set of clubs, but I never really got good at it. But it paid off for me, like I said, because of the Evans Scholarship. They based their selection on three things: financial need, grades, and the amount of time the person has caddied. I wasn't really sure I could get it, but it was sure worth the try."

"I WAS REALLY HOMOPHOBIC"

Now Nikki is a college student at a Big Ten university with a double major, although she says that she enjoys her work in women's studies more than finance. She works part-time, and is active in

Nikki's mother and brother are very supportive of her and her girlfriend, Nicki. Nicki has become a part of the family, receiving presents on holidays and participating in family events.

In order to help other people understand homosexuality, Nikki participates in panel discussions about the subject.

the campus GLBT (Gay, Lesbian, Bisexual, and Transgender) organization as its treasurer. Nikki is obviously very open and confident about her sexuality. Is that because she came out at a fairly early age?

"Actually," says Nikki, shaking her head with an embarrassed smile, "I didn't come out to anybody until my senior year of high school. And that wasn't because I'd been living with the secret for years before that. I honestly didn't know I was a lesbian until senior year. So aside from telling my parents and a very few close friends, I never came out until I came to the university!"

What's funny, says Nikki, is that she was actually homophobic in junior high school.

"I know it sounds very strange coming from a lesbian," she admits, "but I was terrible. I mean, it's not like I was alone in it, or anything. It was pretty common in my school, even in high school. It was the usual dumb stuff you say to get a laugh: Someone brushes against you or touches you or something, and you say something like, 'Get away from me, you homo!' or something to that effect.

"I look back on this now with embarrassment and a lot of confusion. See, I don't know if deep down I knew I was a lesbian then and was just in denial. I don't think that's true, but I can't be sure. I certainly knew that what I was saying wasn't right. It would have been like saying *nigger* or something. But see, if someone said that, teachers would get mad at you, or other kids would give you a look. I never would have said anything racial. But no one even looked at me strangely then, or at any of the kids who said things like that. No one corrected kids for saying queer or homo or anything. No one was critical.

"I also realize now how hurtful that must have been. I mean, my current girlfriend—who is my only girlfriend ever—went to school with me. And although she didn't realize she was a lesbian back then, she certainly must have been embarrassed, because her mother is a lesbian! It's one of those things you do as a kid that you wish you could undo, but you can't."

THE GAME OF LIFE AND *THE BRADY BUNCH*

Nikki says that just recently she was thinking about her teenage years and was wondering if there were signals along the way that she didn't notice until senior year of high school.

"In some ways, I was a tomboy," she says, "although I know there are many, many heterosexual women who were tomboys, too. I liked playing sports instead of dolls. I was a pretty rough-and-tumble kid, but then so were many straight women. I do remember feeling jealous of my brother, because he seemed to have more choices, more fun things to do. In Boy Scouts, they got to do camping and other neat stuff. I hated Girl Scouts because it seemed pretty tame. There were a lot of gender-inequity things that I used to wish weren't so. It always seemed as if it would be more fun to be a boy."

What about childhood fantasies about being a mother, a wife? Nikki laughs.

"I never really thought about getting married or having kids," she says thoughtfully. "I don't remember it, anyway. I know I never sat in class writing my name as Mrs. Tom Smith or whatever. Lots of my friends did that, but I never did.

"My big dream came from two sources," she says. "The first was this game we used to play when we were little, called Life. One of the first things I picked up on in that game was that the two jobs which made the most money were doctor and lawyer. I was really young, but right there I decided that I wanted to be either the doctor or the lawyer.

"The other source of my dream was in an episode of *The Brady Bunch*. Alice in the show made some comment about judges making lots of money, so that steered me more towards law. First a lawyer, I decided, then a judge!"

A JUNIOR HIGH CRUSH

Nikki says that she was recently going through her diary of one of her junior high years, and she found something that she hadn't thought about for years.

"Somewhere in the middle of eighth grade," she says, "I had written that I really had a crush on this one girl. I wrote, 'No, no, I can't really have a crush on her, that can't be! It must be something else.' I must have thought it was wrong in some way, wrong to have that feeling. So what I did was to stow it way, way, way back in my mind. I never dealt with it then. And it wasn't a sexual attraction; it was just a kind of obsession. I wanted her as my friend, even though she already was a friend. I wanted her to be better than the others, like my ultimate friend, or something.

"I never acted on it or anything. I never talked to her about it. That would have been the height of embarrassment. So as I said before, I sensed that it was not appropriate, so I merely filed it far back in my mind."

"OKAY, WE CAN BE LESBIANS"

Nikki says she can pinpoint the moment she first felt a sexual attraction to another girl.

"It was at the beginning of my senior year," she explains. "I was sleeping over at my best friend Nicki's house. Her name is like mine, only spelled with a C-K. Anyway, it was really cold that night, and I sort of wrapped my arm around her to get warm. And all of a sudden, I felt like, wow, this feels really good. We sort of clicked on this intimate level, just kissing a little and cuddling.

"Nicki and I thought about it afterwards. We talked about what that was all about, and we said, 'Oh, no, we're not lesbians. This is a personal thing; we just really like each other.' We figured we were friends, just on some really new level.

"So for about a week we did that. We were denying that we were lesbians, and then after a week we said to each other, 'Okay,

Nikki first realized she was a lesbian during her senior year of high school; however, she did not experience the angst and frustration that most gay teens struggle against.

we can be lesbians. We'll claim that title. But it doesn't mean the same thing it means for other lesbians. We are only attracted to each other, not to other women. It's just us.' And she's been my girlfriend ever since."

Had she gone out with any boys? Did she have any basis for comparison? Nikki nods emphatically.

"I gave guys a try," she says. "I dated a few, and had a pretty good time. I wouldn't say it was a spectacular time, never anything wonderful. I was in England for a while during my junior year, too, and I dated guys over there. It was the same thing—never any relationship that I wanted to last and last. I never felt that with anyone until Nicki."

TELLING FAMILIES

Nikki remembers that coming out to their families was something of an irony.

"If anyone shouldn't have been nervous about telling her parents she was lesbian, it was Nicki," she says. "She had two moms—one was her biological mom who had been married, but it didn't work out. She and her partner had raised Nicki in a very open, honest environment.

"But Nicki was afraid of confronting them. She had seen some television program about a teenaged girl, a lesbian, who had gone to her aunt, I think, for support. The aunt was a lesbian, so she would be understanding, right? But instead of being supportive

Nikki says she has never worried about being different. "So when it comes to being a lesbian, I guess I'd have to say that I can't imagine being any other way."

when the girl came out to her, the aunt tried to talk her out of it, tried to get her to be straight. Nicki was afraid something like that might happen.

"But she shouldn't have worried. Her moms were fine about that. And really, how could they have been otherwise? It was a, like, been-there-done-that kind of thing. They were very understanding, very supportive."

For Nikki, telling her aunt seemed less stressful than telling her parents, at least right away.

"My aunt has always been close to me. I think a lot of times it's easier to talk to someone a little further removed, like maybe a

Nikki receives a flyer at a college rally. She says that one of the most rewarding parts of her college life is working with the gay and lesbian organization on campus.

grandparent or an aunt or someone," she says. "I told my aunt that I was a lesbian. This was about six months into Nicki's and my relationship. Her reaction wasn't one of shock or horror or even disapproval. She just asked me if I was happy, and I assured her that I was.

"Later, she wrote me this big long letter, saying that in some ways my being a lesbian *was* upsetting to her, because of the discrimination and the unkindnesses that gay and lesbian people often experience from the straight community. She just didn't want me to have that kind of hurt in my life, because she loves me."

"I JUST WASN'T READY YET"

Her aunt did not reveal Nikki's confidence to Nikki's mother and father, a fact that both frustrated and pleased Nikki.

"It was so hard bringing it up to my mom," she remembers with a sad smile. "I kept wishing that she would just know, she would just figure it out, and I didn't have to go through that scene."

Nikki interrupts her train of thought for a moment.

"Don't misunderstand," she insists. "It's not that I felt my mom would be hostile or anything. In my brain I knew she would always love me, always support me no matter what. But on an emotional level, I was pretty scared of that kind of a confrontation!

"It is kind of funny, because during my senior year of high school, my mom *did* ask me about it. We were just sitting at home talking about gay and lesbian rights. I'm not sure whether it was something in the newspaper or what, that prompted our talk. Anyway, right in the middle of the conversation, she asked me, 'Nikki, are you a lesbian?'"

Nikki laughs and shakes her head in self-disgust.

"What an opening! All I had to do was tell her! But instead I chickened out. I first said, yes. And then I said no right away and left the room. Just like that. Kind of pathetic, right? I don't know why I couldn't have said yes and shut up, but I didn't. I think now that I just wasn't ready yet. I wasn't as sure of myself as I am today."

"MY BROTHER CRIED A LITTLE"

Nikki was out of high school when she finally told her immediate family.

"I told my mom a year after I found out I was a lesbian," she says. "We were in the car one afternoon, and my brother was in the car, too. Her reaction was no big deal. She kind of knew, I guess, because she'd asked me earlier. My brother cried a little. I don't think he expected that kind of news. He's so sensitive. I think part of his difficulty with it was like my aunt's had been: he was worried I was going to get ridiculed by my friends.

"He dealt with it first by telling his best friend—kind of testing the waters, I think. And then, it was fine. He was kind of forced into having to make some choices that he'd never had to make before, though. Like, what was his reaction when someone told a homophobic joke? I think siblings of kids who come out, especially when they're close in age, have it tough sometimes."

Nikki says that her mother has since surprised her with the degree of acceptance and support she's offered.

"I mean, she still has some reservations about it, even almost two years later," she says. "But she sees it in a different light than what I expected. It's not that she's just *tolerating* my way of life. She told me recently, 'You know, Nikki, for me it's like I was planning on going on this big trip to Asia. But instead, I end up in Africa. It's like I didn't expect to go there, but it's still interesting and new. It's not a question of bad or good. Just different.' I understood what she meant, and that made me feel so good. I can't tell you what a difference it made for me."

THE DO-THE-RIGHT-THING FAMILY

Nikki admits that her father's reaction was neither as supportive nor as understanding as the rest of her family's.

"It was my mom who told my dad. In fact, my mom sort of went on a rampage after I told her, and she told everyone! I mean everybody—the neighbors, the grandparents, our pastor, anybody she thinks should know. I wasn't upset; it actually made it easier for me. But my dad felt really confused, because it was one of a lot of changes I'd been going through.

"See, when I first started college and began taking all these women's studies classes, I went through this stage of being the angry feminist. I think, actually, that that's pretty common when you begin studying something really intensely that really affects you. I mean, every day I'm reading this stuff about how horribly women have been treated through the years, and I was getting angry and frustrated. I wanted to go out and change the world right away.

"Because my dad sort of fits right into that role of white, middle-class, middle-aged man, well, he felt as though he were the target of all my frustration. He took it personally, and that was mostly my fault. Now I've mellowed somewhat, and I can put what I study into perspective, but then I couldn't.

"So anyway, he felt threatened, felt hurt that everything he stood for was a target for me to ridicule, to reject. And for a long time after my mom told him about my being lesbian, he thought that, too, was a backlash against everything he's tried to teach me. It scared him, and like I said, I understand that now."

Nikki maintains that it is a testament to her father's strength that he gradually come to understand her.

"I know that deep down my dad still has some problems with my being a lesbian," she says. "But I also know that he loves me very much. So things will be all right. I know they will. In a way, we've been closer lately, because we have so much to talk about.

"My dad has changed in some ways since this has come up. Like recently, he got in an argument with someone at church about gays and lesbians in the church. He was very much in favor of gay and lesbian people having a bigger role in the running of the church, and I don't think he ever would have said anything like that before.

"But, see, we are a close family. And for whatever reason, we are a kind of do-the-right-thing family. Either we speak up and feel kind of horrible, or we do nothing for a while and feel kind of horrible. We're not always the first to speak out or the first to make the move. But eventually we always seem to get around to doing the right thing."

"PERMANENT, FOREVER"

Nikki's face breaks into a grin when the conversation switches back to her girlfriend, Nicki.

"As I said before, we have been friends so long, I feel like I've known her forever." She smiles. "She's always been a part of my family, sending birthday cards to my grandparents, getting Christmas presents from my mom and dad. It seems like such a natural progression. We talk a lot about our relationship, trying to make it stronger. We both know that college is a time when people change

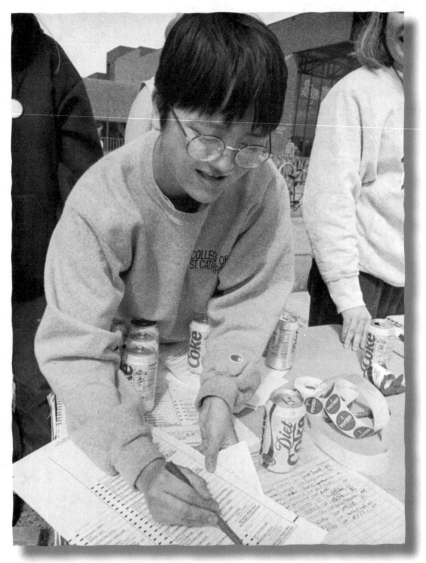

As part of her college involvement, Nikki helps out with the voting booths at the student elections.

a lot, things get all topsy-turvy. But even with all that, we've remained close. Our relationship is closer than it ever has been. I feel right now that we will be permanent, forever."

The two do not go to the same school; Nicki attends a small private college just a few miles away.

"I see her all the time," says Nikki. "She's really active on her campus, the head of this group called WOW—that's Women-Oriented Women. It's much like the GLBT organization that I'm active in. It's harder where she is, though, because organizing in a small Catholic college, it seems like she's always breaking new ground and coming up against a lot of resentment.

"But Nicki doesn't let it get to her," Nikki says with a laugh. "She's this little activist, and she's really cool. She's got support from lots of people, and she's exceptionally good at talking to people without intimidating them or putting them on the defensive. I'm really proud of her.

"She's chosen teaching as her profession, and I'm sure she'll make a good teacher. She's majoring both in Spanish and elementary education. I'll be hopefully raising lots of money for a women's rights organization—that's my plan. I think we'll complement each other. We can roll with whatever comes along."

Helping Out

One of the most rewarding parts of her university life, Nikki says, is her work with the GLBT organization. Not only does it serve as good practice for the kind of work she'll do when she graduates, but she feels that the organization is a good way of reaching out to others in the gay community.

"It's a really multipurpose group," she explains. "I mean, we organize educational programs, we have meetings about activities like National Coming Out Week. We plan social things, too, because it's really difficult for lots of gay and lesbian people who haven't found a group in which they feel comfortable.

"It's funny . . . I've read so many painful stories about junior high and high school kids who suffered through isolation and loss of their peer group when they came out. You'd get the idea that most kids have come out by the time they get to college or at least have dealt with their sexuality in some conscious way. But you'd be surprised at the numbers of kids here—kids my age—who are totally cut off, wondering where they fit in.

"Some of those ask for help, for resources to assist them in coming out to other people, especially their families. Or they just want some activities where they can meet people, other gay or lesbian people like them. It's so much more difficult for them than for heterosexual people. I mean, it's really assumed everywhere that people are all straight, so it's relatively easy for a guy to approach a girl, or vice versa, to plan something to do. I think the straight community just takes the idea of socializing for granted."

GAYDAR

But do gay and lesbian people? It's difficult, says Nikki, since a gay or lesbian person can never assume that another person is also gay. For a young lesbian woman to approach a woman who is straight can lead to embarrassment for the former and sometimes anger or disgust on the part of the latter.

"On the other hand, some gays and lesbians talk about having kind of an intuition about other gay and lesbian people," she says. "Sometimes it's called 'Gaydar,' like gay radar. I'm not sure if there really is a sort of sixth sense that enables all gay and lesbian people to identify another gay or lesbian person. I *am* sure that there are some really good ways of reading people, if you know what to look for."

Nikki rejects the idea that gay men are easy to spot because of their voices, their actions, or their walks or that lesbians stand out in a crowd because of their masculinity.

"Those are stereotypes," she says disdainfully. "They are almost clichés now. I mean, to assume that a man is gay because he doesn't play sports, or to assume a woman is a lesbian because she *does* play sports—that's ridiculous. There are many, many gay and lesbian people that don't display the stereotypical indicators.

"On the other hand, I'm not going to deny that sometimes you just *know*. When Nicki and I first began our relationship in high school, I vividly remember that we became more aware of other kids who we discovered might be gay or lesbian, too. I don't really know how it worked; maybe it wasn't even a conscious thing. But I know I could look at a person in a different way, see a part of myself in her face. I sensed that maybe she was experiencing some of the same feelings I was."

TAKING THE MYSTERY OUT OF IT

Nikki says that even without the mysterious sense about other lesbians she experienced in high school, she knows now that there are some fairly reliable indicators of gay and lesbian people—ones that don't rely on stereotypes or clichés.

"Sometimes it's not based so much on how the person looks as it is the context of where you see the person," she explains. "There are certainly places that you're more likely to find gay and lesbian people, like some of the smaller coffee houses where gay kids go, places they might feel more comfortable. There are also the gay

Nikki and her friend share a warm embrace as they meet on campus.

bars, of course. The bars are probably the most likely indicator that someone is gay, but I'm not a big fan of gay bars. They can be meat markets, the same as any singles bar.

"Sometimes there are verbal clues that indicate if someone is queer, like using the word *partner* instead of someone's assuming a girl has a boyfriend or a boy must have a girlfriend. Or they are interested in talking about some of the issues gay and lesbian people talk about. These aren't foolproof, of course. But the way I see it, even if someone you see talking with gay people or hanging out at a small coffee house isn't gay, at least you're pretty much guaranteed that they are open-minded and supportive. At least that's how I look at it."

What about that word *queer*? Isn't that a derogatory term used by heterosexuals to ridicule gay or lesbian people? Nikki grins and nods.

"It's kind of funny," she says. "I use the word a lot, or I just say Q when I'm talking about a gay or lesbian person. And you're right, it is an insulting term if a heterosexual is using it. I think the gay and lesbian community has sort of reclaimed the word, much like African Americans have reclaimed the word *nigger*. They can use the word referring to themselves or to one another, but it's certainly inappropriate for a white person to use the word. It's wrong, just like a straight person calling me queer. In the community, it's fine, but outside it's hurtful."

"THAT KIND OF STUFF MAKES ME PHYSICALLY SICK"

Nikki's voice has taken on an edge, and she apologizes.

"I get angry sometimes," she says. "There are some things that make me so furious, and even more so when there's nothing I can do about it. I think the angriest I ever was happened at the state fair not long ago. There was this guy wearing a T-shirt that said, 'Silly faggot, dicks are for chicks.' Wearing that at the fair, where everybody was looking at it! I was furious. I kept thinking, why

Nicki was Nikki's first girlfriend. They were great friends, and as their relationship evolved, they thought, "Oh, no, we're not lesbians. This is a personal thing; we just really like each other."

would anyone think that a shirt like that would be appropriate? And who would make those shirts, and who would sell them?

"That kind of stuff makes me physically sick," she says bitterly. "It bothers me so much to see that kind of inequity, seeing people mocking other people, or people being mean to their children, or mean to their spouses. I hate that Congress and the state legislatures can drag their feet when it comes to really important stuff, like health care, or poverty, or homelessness. But when some issue like gay rights or the legality of gay marriages comes up, everybody sure gets energized in a hurry. I mean, why not worry about the things that should have priority?"

A LACK OF INFORMATION

Although she hasn't experienced any of the anguish that many high schoolers suffer when they realize they are gay or lesbian, Nikki says she thinks about those young people a lot.

"One problem I can really identify with is the embarrassment that comes with seeking information," she says. "And that hasn't changed a great deal. I remember when Nicki and I decided we were lesbians, we wanted to find some books or something that would help us a little, help us understand what we were feeling.

"But there's really a big empty space where that information should be. Honestly, the gay issues section of the library was about four books wide! Lots of my gay and lesbian friends have experienced the same things. Nicki and I ended up going to a bookstore and getting a book called *Is It a Choice?* or something like that. It helped, but as I remember, it was all about gay men, not lesbians at all!

"Just buying it was agony, kind of like buying tampons at the grocery store when a boy you know is working at the checkout counter! Nicki and I were careful to put the book face down on the counter so the scanner numbers were up, but not the title. We were so worried that the clerk would see. I guess I figured out eventually that clerks aren't really that interested in what you're buying.

"Anyway, when you start thinking about stuff like that, you realize how difficult it is for lots of gay and lesbian kids. I mean, you have to have enough nerve to go into the bookstore in the first place, and then you have to worry about where you're going to hide it when you get home!"

Nikki is very active in college programs and has met many people through the different organizations that stand up for student rights.

OPEN OR SECRET?

How does that nervousness, that sense of secrecy finally disappear? For many gay and lesbian people, she says, it doesn't.

"It's always a thought in the back of your mind," she insists. "No matter how open you are, how friendly and courteous you are, no matter how qualified or talented you are, there is always the possibility that you will be discriminated against simply because you are gay or lesbian.

"I'd be astonished if I thought it would affect me in the line of work I want to pursue. I mean, how worried would a gay activist organization be that their financial manager was a lesbian? But for people in most lines of work, it can be an issue.

"Take Nicki; she's going to be a teacher. Now in this state, we've got some really good antidiscrimination laws that prohibit an employer from disqualifying an applicant for being gay. But we aren't naive enough to think that's much protection. A law is only as tough as its enforcement. If someone on a school board somewhere doesn't like it that Nicki's a lesbian, there are lots of reasons he or she could keep her from working, even if that reason isn't important. Even if she's the most qualified teacher out there, she could be fired, or not hired in the first place. It's not much different from what African Americans have experienced for many years."

"I WANT TO BE AS HONEST WITH PEOPLE AS I CAN"

Some gay and lesbian people opt for hiding that aspect of their lives, Nikki says, to protect themselves from such discrimination or from the disapproval of others. But in doing that, they are right back in a position of being in the closet.

"I want to be as honest with people as I can," she says. "My own feeling is that the more I can show people that I'm not so different from them, that I'm not abnormal, they can learn to be more accepting.

Nikki enthusiastically claps her hands and cheers during a college rally. By participating in college programs and clubs, Nikki has helped to open the minds of her peers and teach them about homosexuality.

"Take my roommate situation. I don't choose my roommates, they're chosen for me here [at college]. All of my roommates have been straight. I was nervous about how they would feel when I told them I was a lesbian. Never did I really consider keeping it hidden. A couple of them were really staunch Christians, but that didn't completely worry me, because Nicki is, too! But these girls didn't really agree with my way of life and said so.

"So we talked about it. I was upset a little bit that they were judging me before they really knew me. But it ended up to be fine. They were fair. We've ended up being friends. They've been respectful and understanding about me. We talk, we are open. And Nicki comes around a lot, and that helps. They can see we're really normal, not threatening in the least. No public displays of affection—I can't stand that from straight people either! I guess the more you know people, the easier it is to be tolerant of different ideas."

HELPFUL WORDS FROM HIGH SCHOOL

Has she ever secretly wished she were not a lesbian, that things in her life were easier?

"No, never," she says with an honest smile. "I have pretty good self-esteem. I like myself. I have plenty of faults, but they have nothing to do with being a lesbian. That's just part of me.

"I've never worried about being different, and that's been a plus for me. I was always lousy at putting on makeup, so somewhere back in high school I gave up trying. And I'm really bad at figuring out what outfits look best on me or what goes with what. So I wear what's comfortable. I've never been one to worry about buying the right jeans or having the shoes everyone else is buying.

"So when it comes to being a lesbian, I guess I'd have to say that I can't imagine being any other way. I love Nicki; I love my friends—straight and gay. I've been forced to learn about things like tolerance and politics and social troubles. Taking classes about issues like these, reading books and having discussions about gay and lesbian issues, I feel like I'm informed and educated, and that's good. It helps you keep a positive attitude about who you are and what you're doing.

"I had a teacher in high school who sensed that I was a lesbian, long before Nicki and I had told anyone. I was talking to this teacher about another friend who had come out, and how the kids were treating her so badly. Anyway, I looked at this teacher, and I had the feeling she knew exactly what I was feeling: that even though I was talking about this friend, I was also thinking about myself.

"All of a sudden she looked right at me and said, 'You know, Nikki, you're going to be fine.' It was so great, hearing those words. I believed her, what she said. And I've thought about it lots of times since. She was right."

Epilogue

In the months since the four young people in this book were interviewed, their lives have changed.

Joe has had a run of bad luck, he says. Assured by his mother that she was finally off drugs, he moved back home. However, it was not long before he realized the situation at home had not changed at all. He moved out, and, having no place to stay, he was sleeping in his car. Because he did not have a more suitable home, Joe often overslept and was late for his job at the gay and lesbian center. At present, he is living in a shelter, but he wants to look for a job and rent an apartment. He is not yet back in school.

Nikki has finished another year at the university, and has done well in her classes. Although she is eager to start more classes, she is looking forward to spending more time at home, especially with her brother, who is home from college. She and her girlfriend, Nicki, are still a couple.

Tori and her girlfriend have split up, she says, because "we just didn't have time for each other," as they each got busier and more involved in school and work. Tori is still living at her grandmother's house and has no immediate plans to move out. Her summer softball league was cancelled, but she says she is excited about basketball starting in a month or so. She spends her evenings doing vocals in a hip-hop group that is in its formative stages.

Justin and Larry don't see each other anymore. Justin says that they just drifted apart, but he's not sad about it. He is no longer working at the same job; instead, he works twenty-four hours each weekend at a home for mentally challenged adults—a job which he really enjoys. He graduated from his alternative high school, but has no set plans for next year.

Ways You Can Get Involved

THERE ARE MANY WAYS YOUNG READERS CAN BECOME INVOLVED IN HELPING TO MAKE SOCIETY LESS HOSTILE AND MORE OPEN TOWARD GAY AND LESBIAN YOUTH:

■ Talk to counselors and examine ways to improve your student body's reaction to gay teens.

■ Ask your principal how a support group for gay, lesbian, and bisexual students can be organized at your school.

■ Volunteer to answer phones at a local hotline for troubled teens.

■ Examine yourself and your social group. Are there fellow students who seem to feel left out or who are shunned by others? Do you tolerate others who make gay jokes, or single out others for ridicule?

■ Organize a poster campaign celebrating diversity at your school. Include homosexuality in addition to more easily identified groups, such as African Americans, Native Americans, and people with handicaps.

■ Write to the following organizations for publications that are free to interested readers:

Ministry of Light
1000 Sir Francis Drake Blvd.
San Anselmo, CA 94690
Nonjudgmental ministry within the gay and lesbian community. It offers resources and support to schools, churches, synagogues, families, and social service agencies.

National Coalition of Black Lesbians and Gays
19641 W. Seven Mile
Detroit, MI 48219

Combats racial and sexual oppression through education and newsletters.

National Gay and Lesbian Task Force (NGLTF)
Anti-Violence Project
1517 U Street NW
Washington, DC 20009
The NGLTF raises awareness of anti–gay and lesbian violence and works for support services for victims of violence.

Parents and Friends of Lesbians and Gays (P-FLAG)
PO Box 20308
Denver, CO 80220
This organization sponsors meetings, provides speakers to schools and organizations, and distributes a monthly newsletter.

For Further Reading

Loren Acker, Bram C. Goldwater, and William H. Dyson, *AIDS-Proof Your Kids: A Step-by-Step Guide*. Hillsboro, OR: Beyond Words Publishers, 1992. A no-nonsense guide for parents and kids, with plain and direct answers about the way AIDS is transmitted. Contains good ideas of how parents can help direct school discussions of risk behaviors.

Susan Cohen and Daniel Cohen, *When Someone You Know Is Gay*. New York: M. Evans and Co., 1989. A practical, interesting book written for straight teens on the subject of homosexuality. Excellent section on the dangers of AIDS aimed at gay teens.

Hila Colman, *Happily Ever After*. New York: Scholastic, 1986. A novel for teens and young adults about a gay seventeen-year-old boy and the girl who loves him.

Ann Heron, *One Teenager in Ten*. New York: Warner Books, 1983. A highly readable collection of autobiographical essays by gay and lesbian teens.

Index

About the Author

Gail B. Stewart is the author of more than eighty books for children and young adults. She lives in Minneapolis, Minnesota, with her husband Carl and their sons Ted, Elliot, and Flynn. When she is not writing, she spends her time reading, walking, and watching her sons play soccer.

Although she has enjoyed working on each of her books, she says that *The Other America* series has been especially gratifying. "So many of my past books have involved extensive research," she says, "but most of it has been library work—journals, magazines, books. But for these books, the main research has been very human. Spending the day with a little girl who has AIDS, or having lunch in a soup kitchen with a homeless man—these kinds of things give you insight that a library alone just can't match."

Stewart hopes that readers of this series will experience some of the same insights—perhaps even being motivated to use some of the suggestions at the end of each book to become involved with someone of the Other America.

About the Photographer

Twenty-two-year-old Natasha Frost has been a photographer for *The Minnesota Daily*, the University of Minnesota's student newspaper, for three and a half years. She currently attends the University of Minnesota and is studying sociology and journalism.

When not working at the paper or going to school, Frost enjoys traveling. "It gives me a chance to meet different people and expand my knowledge about the world."